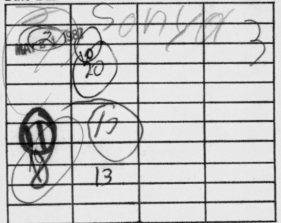

CARD AND CARDBOARD

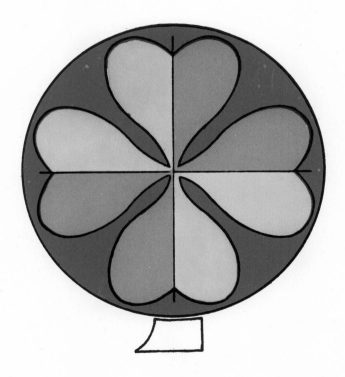

Franklin Watts, Inc
845 Third Avenue
New York, N.Y. 10022

First published October 1969
First English edition 1970
First American publication 1971 by Franklin Watts, Inc.

© 1969 Santillana, S.A. de Ediciones
English translation © 1970, Macdonald & Co. (Publishers) Ltd.

Library of Congress Catalog Card Number: 71-158980

Printed in Spain

Impreso en España, en los talleres
ALVI, Industrias Gráficas,
Manuel Luna, 5, MADRID-20
Depósito Legal: M. 14.123-1971

SBN 531 02002-9

Working with card and cardboard

The projects in this book are divided into five grades, from very simple to advanced. The colour key below shows the grades and corresponding symbols, which are repeated at the beginning of each project for easy reference. The very simple projects are designed for younger children but the grades are only intended as a rough guide. Very young children may need some help.

 **Very simple**

 **Easy**

 **Moderately easy**

 **More complex**

 **Advanced**

Card and cardboard, the second volume in the *Colour Crafts* series, tells you how to make over sixty models. Each project is illustrated with step-by-step colour pictures and photographs.

The colour-coded squares at the beginning of each project will tell you how complex each one is. The earlier projects, intended for younger children, concentrate on the use of card. The more advanced projects make full use of cardboard, as older children should have no difficulty in cutting and handling the thicker material.

Use any standard glue for these models. It is a good idea to hold the sticking surfaces together firmly with paper clips or hair pins while the glue dries. Meanwhile you can get on with other parts of the model. Glue is not always needed. Parts of some models can often be slotted or stapled together.

Some of the models in this book show the parts in the actual size you will need them. All you need to do is trace the outline on to the card or cardboard. A good way is to lay a sheet of tracing paper over the pattern in the book and trace the outline in pencil. Then rub coloured chalk or pencil over the back of the tracing paper. Lay the tracing paper on your sheet of card and go over the pencil outline, pressing quite hard. Take the tracing paper away and you will find your outline in coloured chalk on the card.

Each project gives a list of materials you will need, and it is a good idea to prepare everything before you begin. Always try to keep your work table clean and tidy. As soon as you have made a few models in the book, see if you can invent other models and shapes. You can experiment with different types of materials, colours and designs. If you get stuck, go on to another model and come back to the hard one later.

Some of the models in the book require silver or gold metallic card. If you cannot find these, you can use heavy silver or gold paper, or thinner gold and silver paper stuck on to plain card to make it stiff.

MOUSE

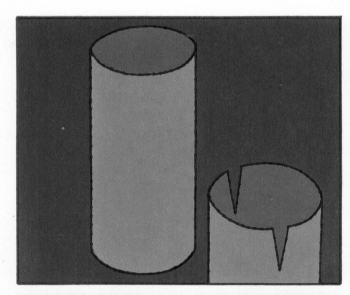

Find an old cardboard tube. Make two slits at the top.

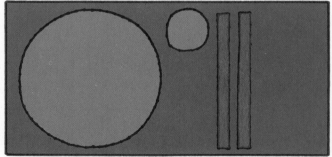

Cut a big circle and a little one out of the green card.
Cut two equal pieces of black raffia.

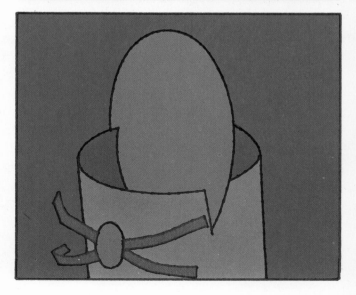

Put the big circle into the two slits that you have made in the tube. Cross the pieces of raffia and glue on to the tube to make the whiskers. Stick the little green circle in the middle of the cross for the nose.

Draw the eyes and the feet
of the mouse with a black
felt-tip pen.

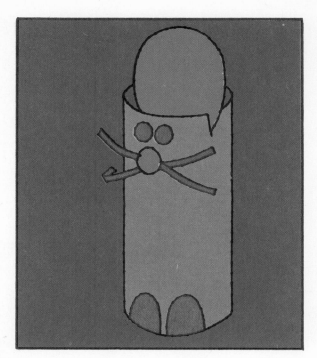

SIMPLE BASKET

Cut out a long strip of blue card and another of yellow card. Cross and glue them together as shown in the picture.

Cut out a circle of red card and stick this in the middle of the cross.

Cut out a wide strip of green card slightly longer than the outside edge of the red circle. Glue the blue and yellow strips on to the outside of the green strip.

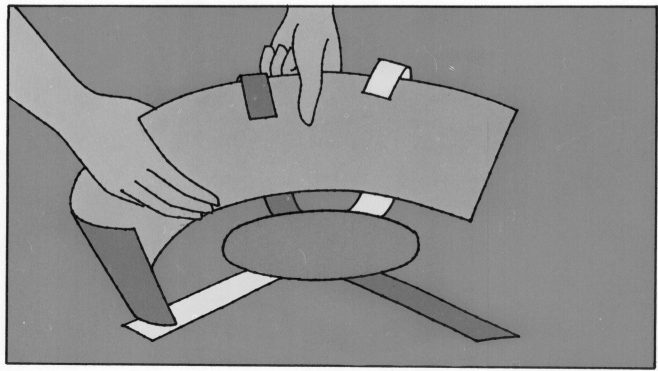

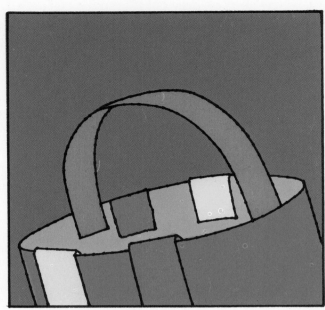

Stick on another strip of card to make a handle.

THE THREE WISE MEN

Draw three squares on different coloured card and cut out.

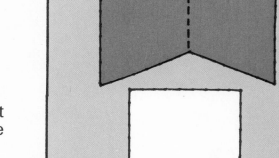

Fold the squares in half. Cut a slit at the left and right hand sides of the top edges.

Draw and cut out three rectangles of white card half as wide as the coloured squares. Make two slits in each as shown.

Use a black felt-tip pen to draw the faces of the Three Wise Men on the rectangles.

Mount the faces by pushing the slits at the bottom of the rectangles over the slits at the top of the squares.

MATERIALS:

- Cardboard
- Darning needle
- Black raffia
- Silver button
- Thin wire
- Black and brown felt-tip pens
- Pencil and scissors

CAT

Cut out a rectangle of cardboard.

Draw part of a cat's face at one end. Draw it in pencil first, then with a felt-tip pen. Cut round the ears.

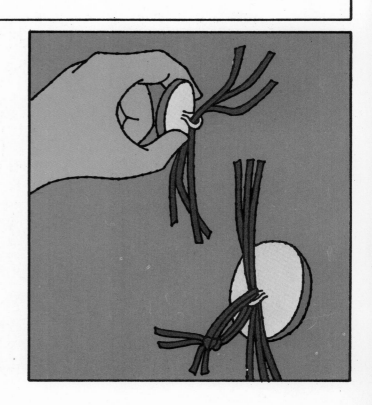

Cut three pieces of black raffia to make the whiskers. Thread them through the loop at the back of a silver button.

Cut three longer pieces of black raffia. Thread them through the button loop. Tie a knot at one end.

Thread the other ends of the raffia through a darning needle.

Push the needle through the cat's face and then through the other end of the cardboard. Pull the raffia tight. The cardboard will bend into a curve. Tie another knot in the raffia to keep the shape of the curve.

Plait the three loose ends of raffia, working in a piece of thin wire as you plait. The plait forms the tail, which the wire will hold firm. Finish off the plait with a knot.

MATERIALS:
● Blue card
● Scissors
● Black felt-tip
  pen
● Pencil

SNAKE

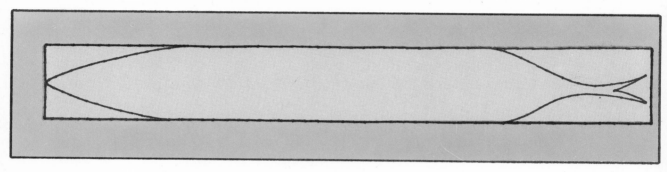

Draw the outline of the snake on a strip of blue card.

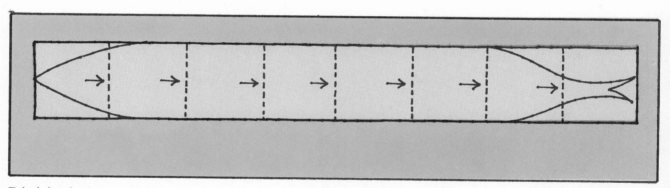

Divide it into eight equal parts, starting with the tail. Cut round the outline.

Fold the strip along the dividing lines, following the direction of the arrows.

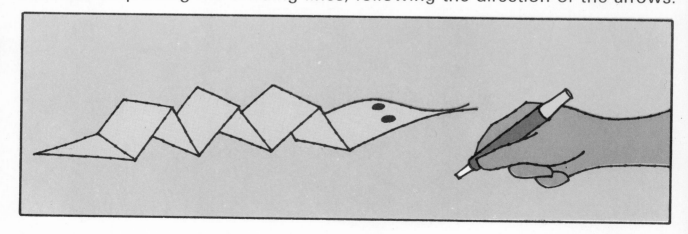

Draw the eyes and tongue with a black felt-tip pen.

MATERIALS:
- **Different coloured card**
- **Scissors**
- **Glue**

WOVEN BASKET

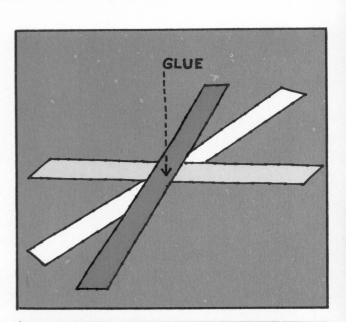

Cut three equal strips of card in different colours.

Put one on top of the other to make a star and stick them together.

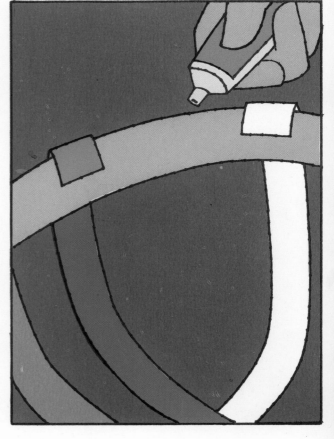

Cut three more long strips of different coloured card.

Stick the ends of one of these together to make a circle.

Now stick the ends of the first strips to the circular strip.

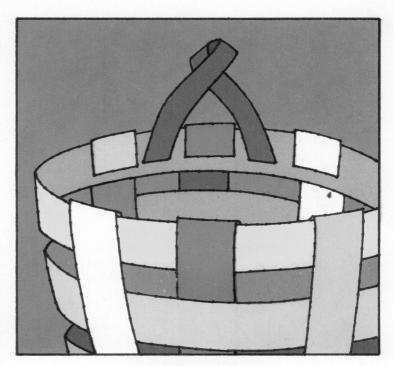

Weave in the other two strips. Finish the basket with two handles made of card.

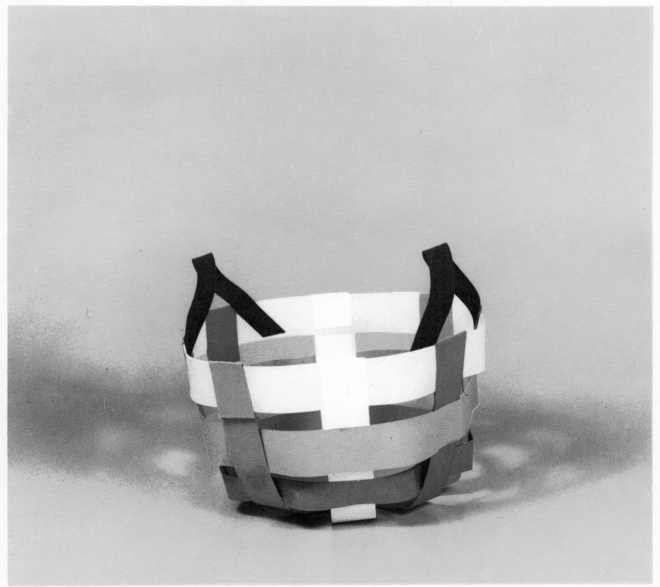

CHICKENS

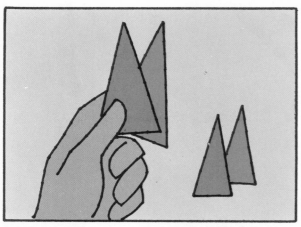

Cut out a circle of green card.

Cut out two triangles in red card for the beak.

Cut out two slightly smaller triangles to make the tail.

Make an eye by sticking a small black circle of card on a white circle. The chicken has an eye on each side.

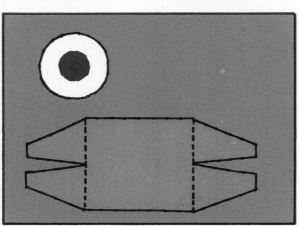

Cut a shape as shown out of red card for the feet.

Fold along the dotted lines.

Stick the pieces on the body as shown. Take the triangles for the beak and stick on either side of the chicken's face. Stick the free ends of the triangles together. Stick the tail on in the same way.

Make the small chicken in the same way, but with smaller pieces of card.

MATERIALS:

- Cardboard
- Light blue card
- Scissors
- Pencil
- Tracing paper
- Glue

SIMPLE SCULPTURE

Cut three triangles like this one out of cardboard.

Cut six circles like the one in the picture out of blue card.

Stick a circle in the centre of both sides of the triangles.

Make the cuts shown below in the triangles. All the cuts must be the same depth.

Slot triangle A on to triangles B and C.

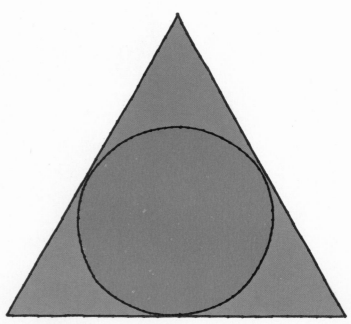

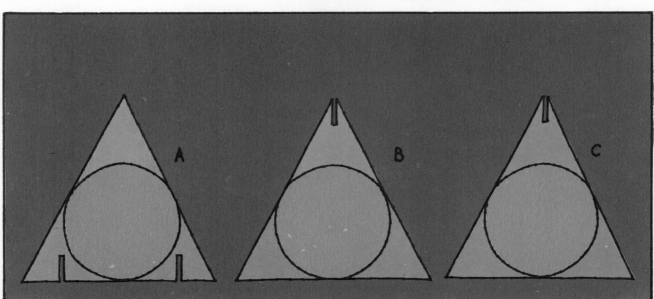

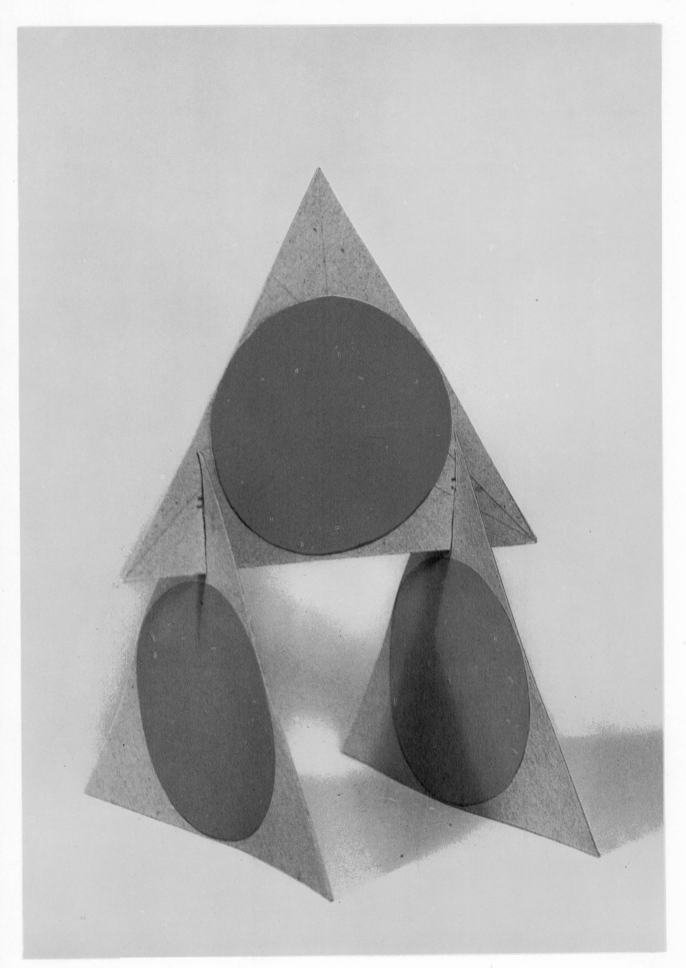

23

MATERIALS:

- Coloured card
- Green felt-tip pen
- Scissors
- Glue

FOREST

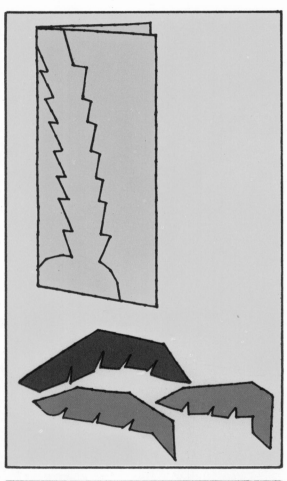

Cut a rectangle out of brown card. Fold it in half. Draw the trunk of a palm tree and cut it out. Cut the leaves out of green card.

Stick the leaves between the top ends of the trunk.

Stick the sides of the trunk together. Leave the bottom open so the palm tree will stand up.

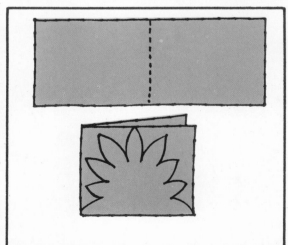

Cut a rectangle out of green card. Fold it in half. Draw a bush and cut it out. Open the card. You can stand the bush in front of the palm tree, or use it as a separate decoration.

Draw a cactus on blue card. Cut it out. Decorate it with a felt-tip pen. Glue a small green bush to the base of the cactus. Fold the cactus to make it stand upright.

You can make other forest plants using the same shapes but different coloured card.

FURNITURE

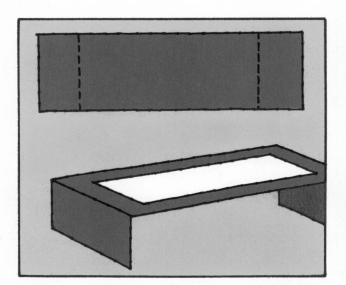

Cut a rectangle out of black card. Fold along the dotted lines to make a table. Cut a small rectangle out of white card and glue it to the top of the table.

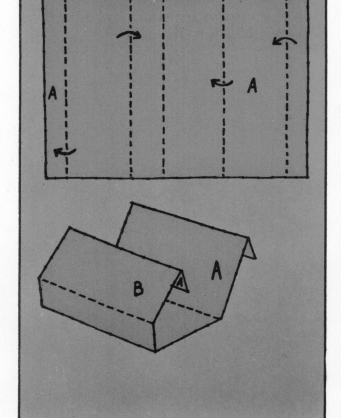

To make a chair, cut a rectangle out of red card. Fold it along the dotted lines. Glue the narrow flap A to the wider section A.

Make the sofa in the same way, starting with a rectangle of the same length but wider.

26

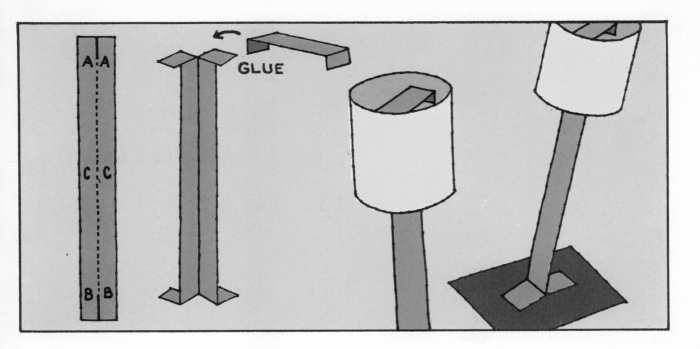

Cut a long, narrow strip out of brown card. Make a cut at the top and bottom. Fold the strip along the dotted line. Then fold the end pieces A and B outwards, and stick C to C.

Now cut out a short strip of brown card and fold over the ends. Glue this strip on to A. Stick the ends to the inside of a lampshade made from yellow card. Stick B on a rectangle of black card.

Make the carpet from a rectangle of green card and cut fringes. Draw a black border with a felt-tip pen.

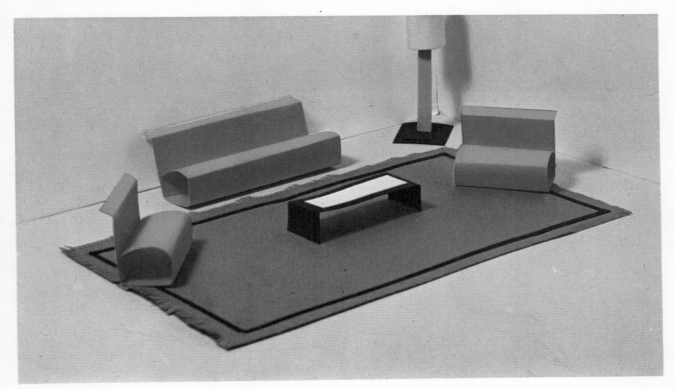

SNAKE

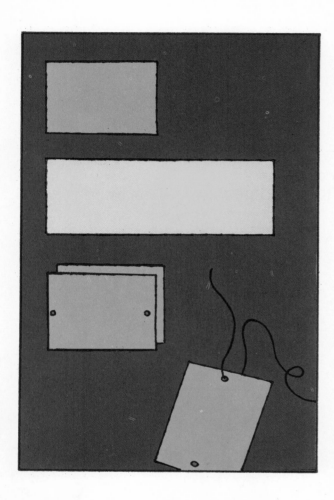

Cut four rectangles out of green card. Cut three more rectangles the same size out of pink card.

Cut out a pink rectangle longer than the others but the same width.

Place the small rectangles on top of each other and make a hole at each end with a needle.

Thread the needle with fine string. Tie a knot at one end and thread the other through the holes, alternating the colours of the rectangles.

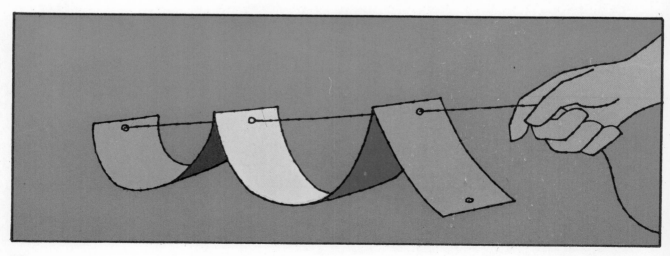

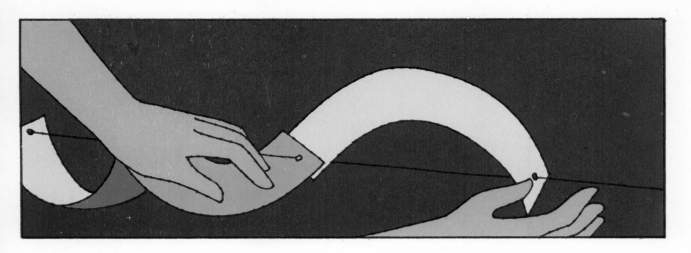

When you have done this, thread the string through the big rectangle, in the position shown in the picture.

Pull the string fairly tight and tie a knot.

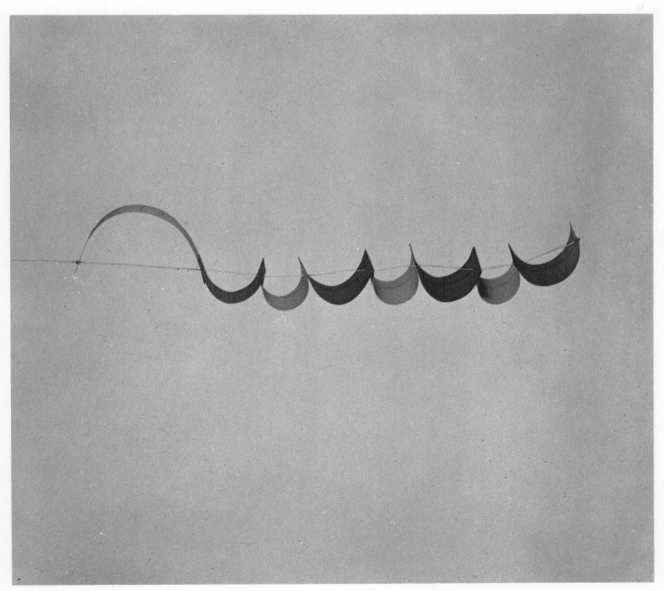

WORKING WITH CIRCLES

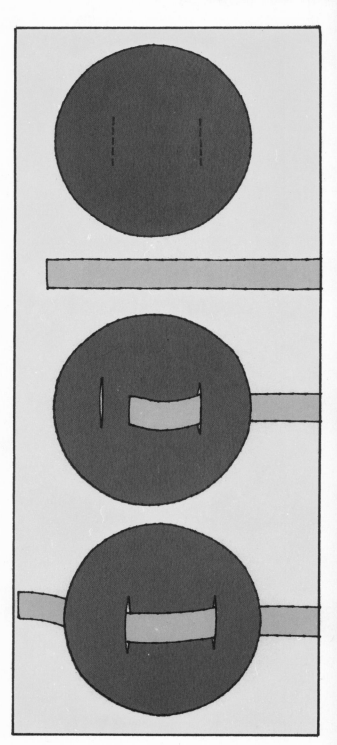

Cut several circles out of black card and cut along the dotted lines.

Cut out a strip of green card that will fit into the slits you have just made.

Thread the strip through the back of the first slit and into the front of the second slit. Pull the circle along to the far end of the green strip.

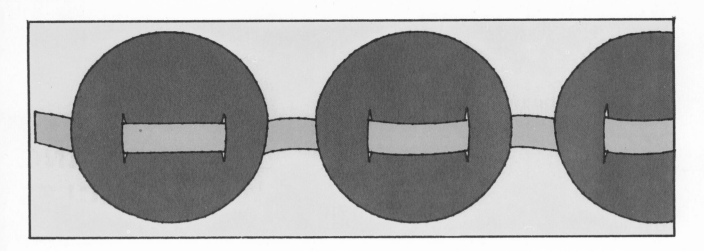

Thread the other circles in the same way. Leave the same amount of space between each.

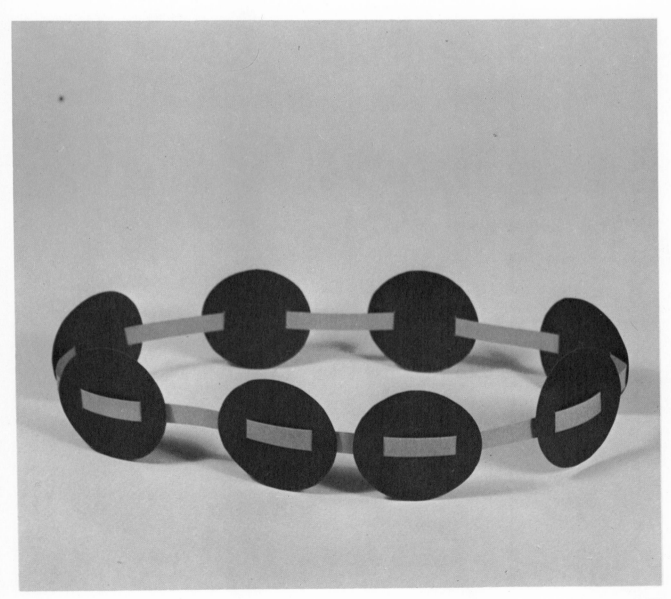

MATERIALS:

- Six cardboard tubes
- Three jars
- Powder paint
- Paint brush
- Water
- Small piece of material
- Scissors

TUBE SCULPTURE

Mix some black powder paint with a little water in a jar. In another jar mix some pink powder paint, and, in another, light blue. Paint three tubes like the one in picture 1.

Paint the other three as shown in picture 2. Wash the paint brush in clean water and dry it on a piece of material every time you use a different colour.

Put the first three tubes side by side, leaving a small space between them. Put another two on top of them. Make a mark where they touch and then cut slits.

Slot the top two tubes on to the bottom three.

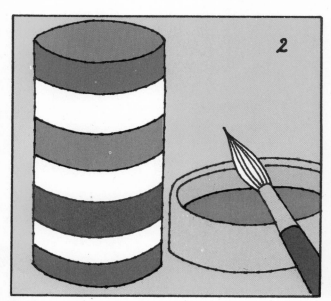

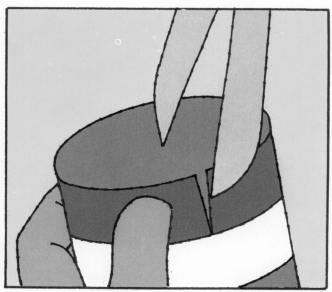

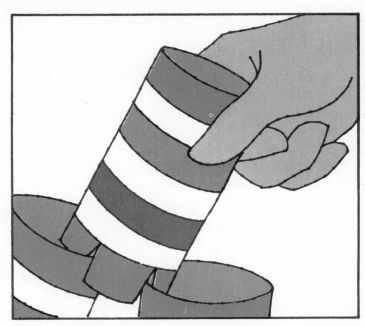

Balance the last tube on the top two. Cut slits at the bottom so that it will fit on the top.

33

MATERIALS:

- Seven small boxes of different sizes
- Black card
- Scissors
- Glue
- Powder paint and brush
- Jars for water
- Piece of material

GIRAFFE

Collect seven empty cardboard boxes of different sizes.

One for the body (1)
Two for the back legs (2)
Two for the front legs (3)
One for the neck (4)
One for the head (5)

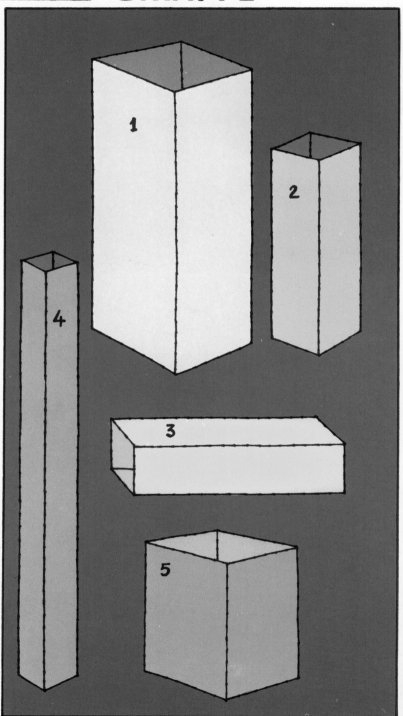

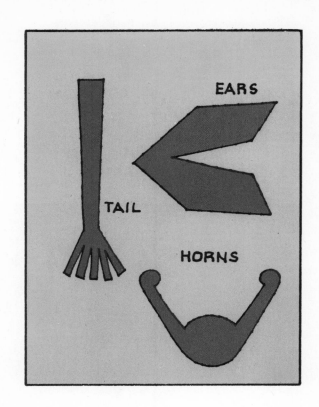

Cut the ears, horns and tail out of black card.

Cut a strip as long as the neck box out of black card. Fold along the dotted lines, following the direction of the arrows.

Cut fringes as shown

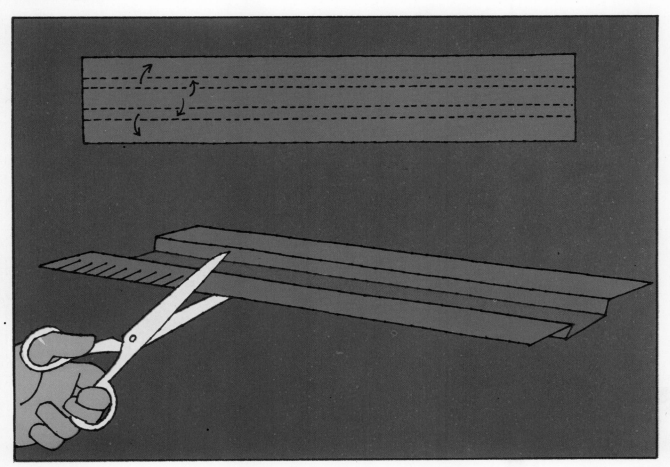

Glue each piece to its box. Then glue the boxes together. Mix some yellow powder paint with a little water. In another jar mix some brown powder paint. Paint the giraffe yellow. When it is dry, paint brown spots on it. Wash the paint brush and dry it on a piece of material every time you use a different colour, and before putting it away.

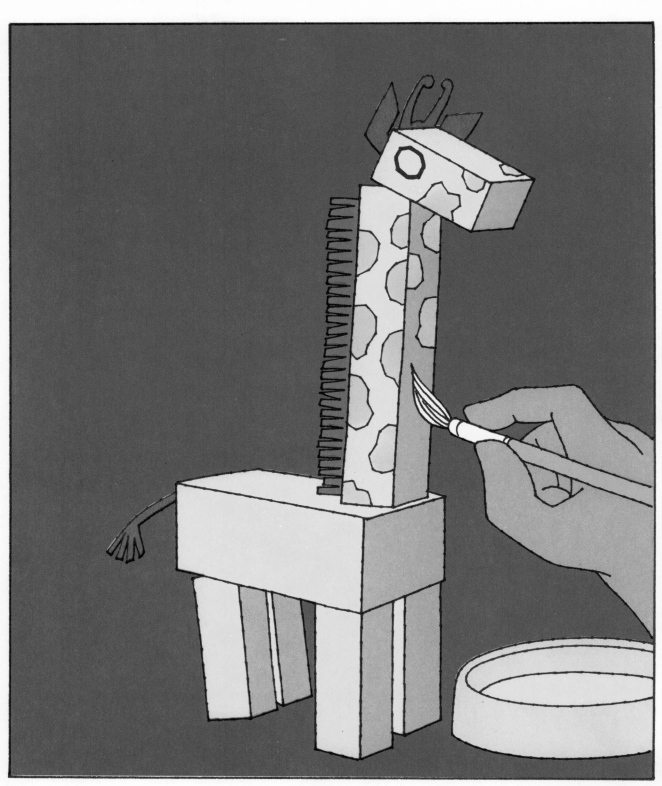

ELEPHANT AND BEAR

Fold a piece of grey card in half and draw an elephant on it. Cut it out through both thicknesses. Cut two ears like the one shown out of grey card.

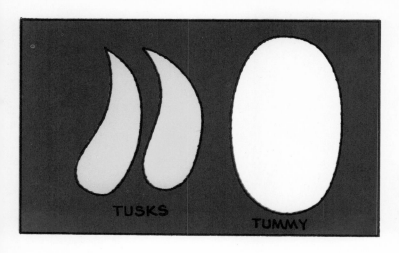

Cut two tusks out of yellow card.
Cut two pieces as shown for the
tummy of the elephant out of
white card.

Glue the ears, tusks and white tummy pieces on to the body as shown.

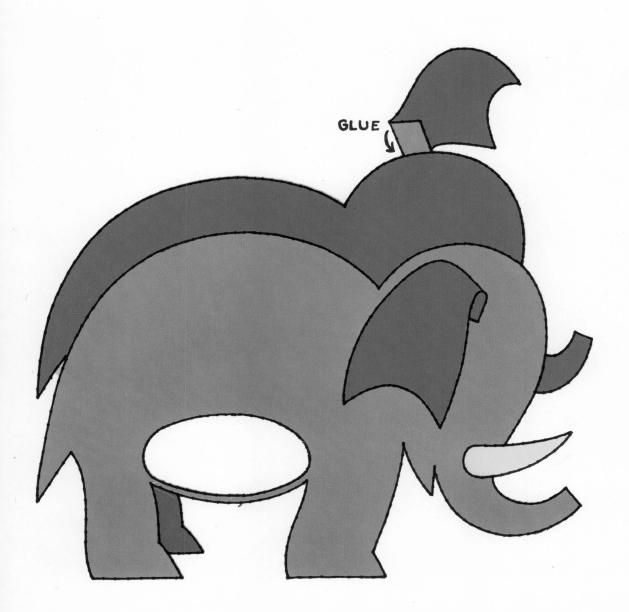

GLUE

Glue the two parts of the elephant together, leaving the feet unstuck. You can make the elephant stand up by bending the legs out a little. Do not glue the ends of the two tusks together, nor the flaps of the ears. Paint in the toes, eyes and nostrils with a brown felt-tip pen.

GLUE

To make a bear, cut two shapes as shown out of brown card.

Cut a circle for the face out of orange card. Cut the nose, eyes and mouth out of black, white and red card as shown.

Stick these on to the face. Glue the face on one of the two body shapes you have cut out.

Cut out a white piece of card as shown and stick it on the tummy of the same body shape as the one you have stuck the face on to.

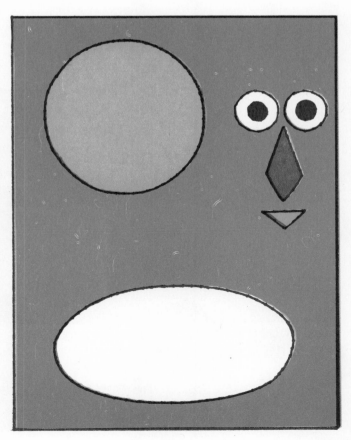

GLUE

Glue together the two shapes you have cut out for the body of the bear, but leave the feet unstuck.

Paint in the toes and the ears with a black felt-tip pen.

You can make other animals in the same way.

43

LION

Fold a piece of light brown card in half. Trace the outline shown on to the card. Cut out the shape.

Trace the outline of the face on to another piece of light brown card.

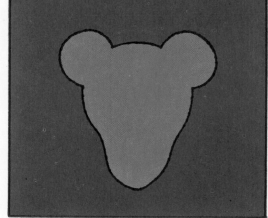

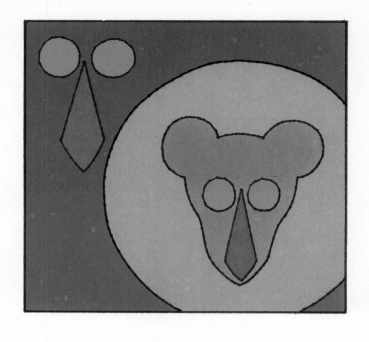

Cut two round eyes out of green card and a nose out of black card.

Stick these on to the face.

Cut a circle as shown out of orange card. Glue the face on to this circle.

Glue the orange circle with the face on to the round shape on one of the sides of the body. Glue the two sides of the body together, leaving unstuck the parts below the dotted line shown in the picture.

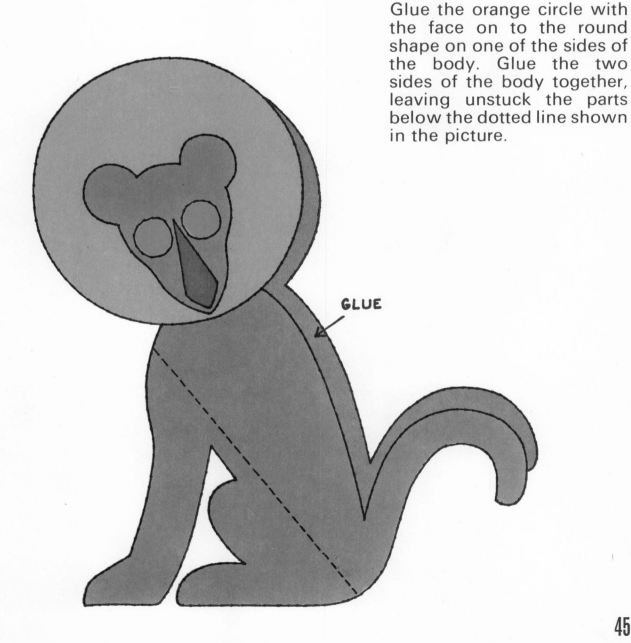

GLUE

Cut fringes round the face as shown. This will make the lion's mane.

Finish the lion by drawing in the claws, the pupils of the eyes, the ears, tail, etc., with a felt-tip pen.

The lion will sit up if you bend the parts which were not stuck together apart slightly.

MOBILE

Cut two identical rectangles out of the same coloured card to make the top (A) and bottom (B) of the mobile.

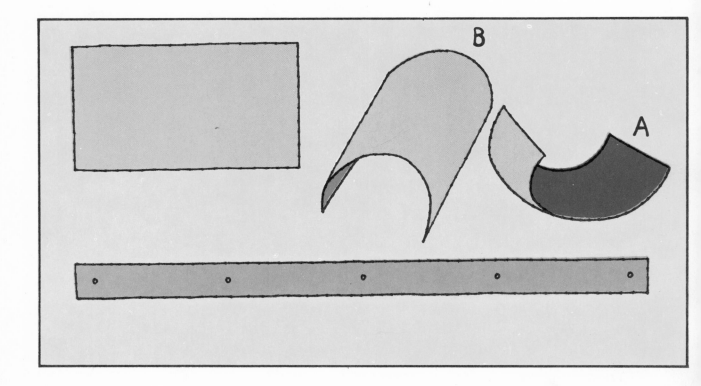

Cut a long strip out of card of another colour, about a third as wide as the other two rectangles.

Mark the strip with dots starting very near one end. Leave a space the width of the large rectangles between each one.

Thread a needle with thin string and pull through the centre of the bottom rectangle (B). Make a knot at the end of the string.

Thread the string through the pencil dots. Complete the mobile with the rectangle A and make a knot in the string.

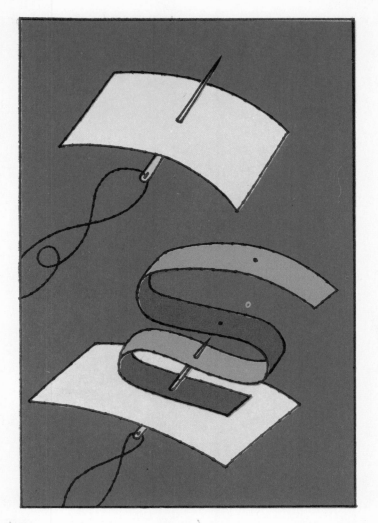

NAPOLEON'S HAT

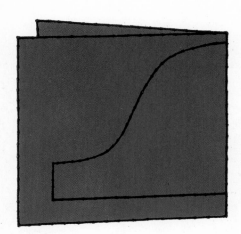

Draw this shape on a piece of folded paper. Cut out.

Open out the paper pattern and draw round it on two pieces of black card. Cut out.

Cut two strips out of white tissue paper to fit round the top edge of the hat. Cut fringes in the strips and stick one on the inside of each black piece.

Now staple the sides of the hat.

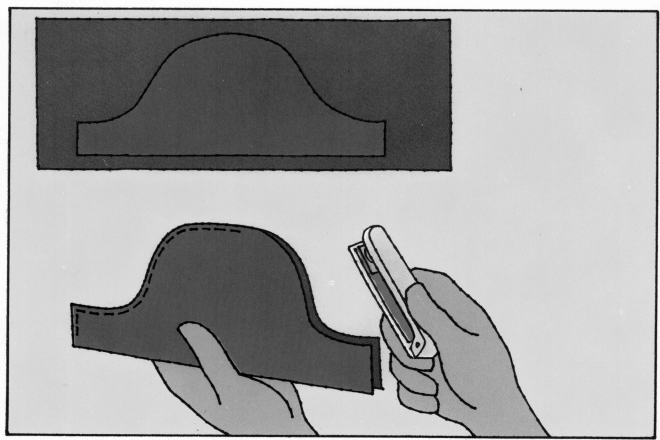

Cut some strips out of blue tissue paper. Fold them in half and stick the ends on to the front of the hat like a rosette. Stick a piece of pink card in the middle.

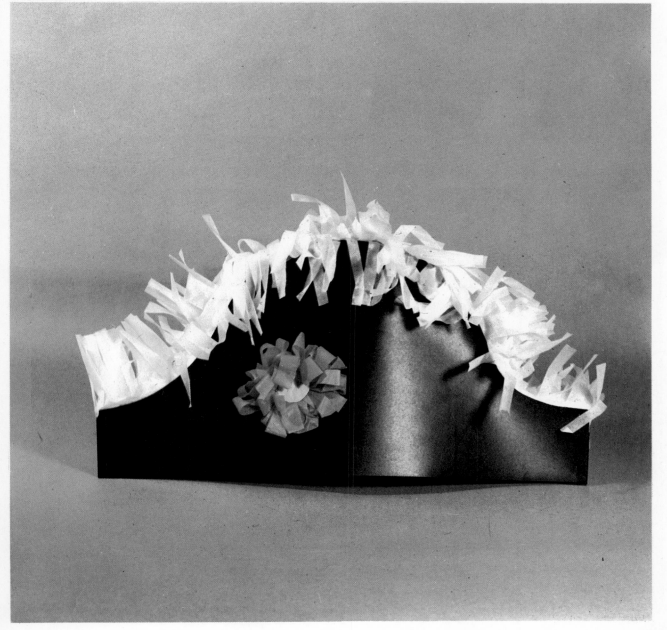

SHIP

Cut out five strips of card in the colours and sizes shown. Make the cuts and folds on each strip as shown in the diagram. The cuts are marked with solid lines and the folds with dotted lines.

Fold in the direction of the arrows. The cuts are half the width of the strips of card.

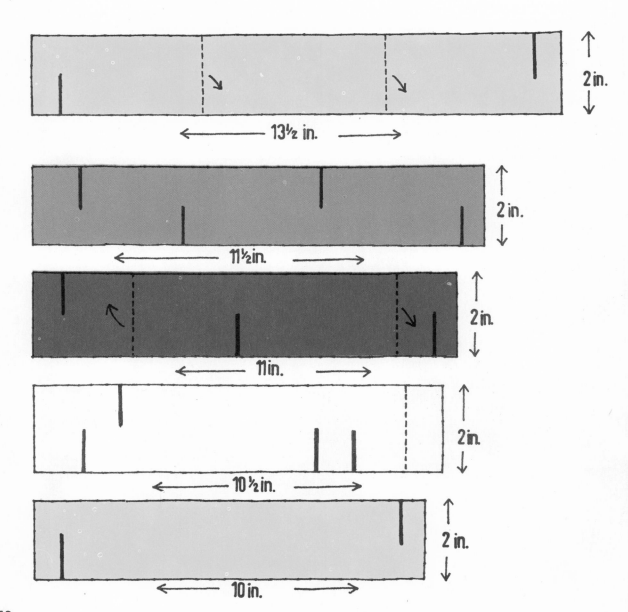

2 in.

13½ in.

2 in.

11½ in.

2 in.

11 in.

2 in.

10½ in.

2 in.

10 in.

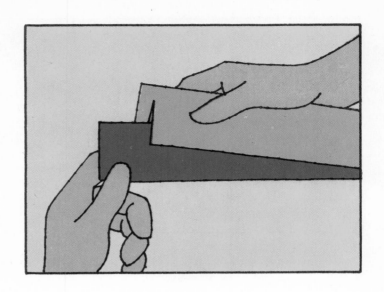

Slot the strips together. The picture shows you where to put each colour strip.

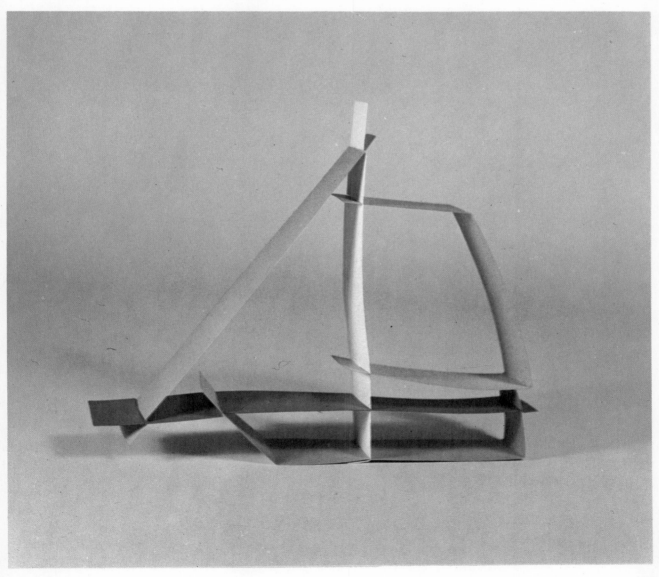

SCULPTURE

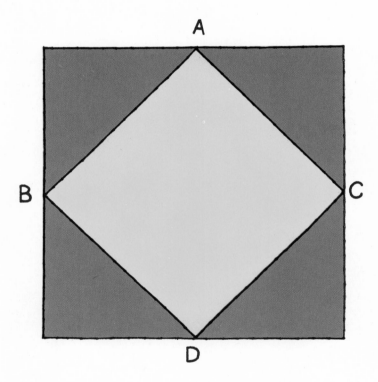

Cut six 5in. squares out of cardboard.

Mark the middle of every edge in pencil.

Join points A, B, C and D to make a new square. Do this on all six squares.

Mix the powder paint with a little water and paint the middle squares. Use a different colour for each one. Clean the paint brush with water and dry it on a piece of material every time you use a different colour.

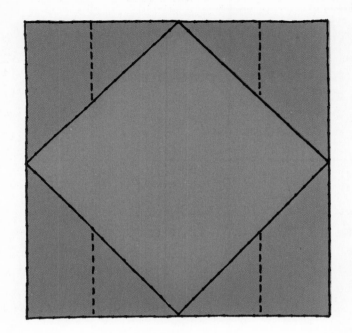

Cut along the dotted lines
on two of the squares. Only
make the cuts at the top
on the other four. Slot the
squares together, using the
picture as a guide.

MATERIALS:

- ● **Different coloured card**
- ● **Ruler**
- ● **Pencil**
- ● **Scissors**

MOBILE OF SEMICIRCLES

Cut a strip of light blue card 2in. wide.

Make cuts about 2in. apart. The cuts should only go to the middle of the strip.

Cut strips of different coloured card 11½in. long and 2in. wide. Make a cut ¾in. from either end on all of them.

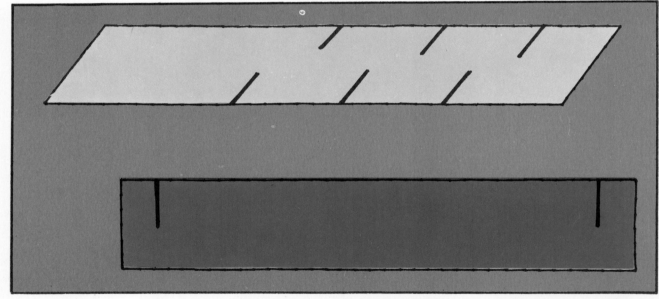

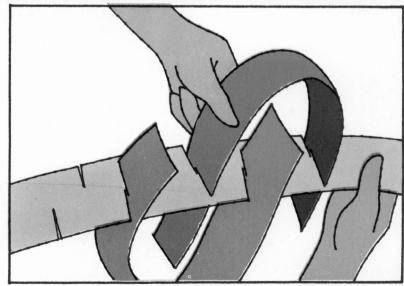

Now slot these strips on to the first one.

ROBOT

Try to find boxes in these sizes so that the model is in proportion.

Sizes:

Head: $3\frac{1}{2}$ by $1\frac{3}{4}$ by $1\frac{3}{4}$in.

Body: $3\frac{1}{2}$ by $3\frac{1}{2}$ by $1\frac{1}{2}$in.

Legs, feet, arms and neck: $3\frac{1}{2}$ by $\frac{3}{4}$ by $\frac{3}{4}$in.

Cut a $\frac{3}{4}$in. square out of the bottom of the head. Put a spot of glue on one end of the neck and push it through the hole to the top of the head.

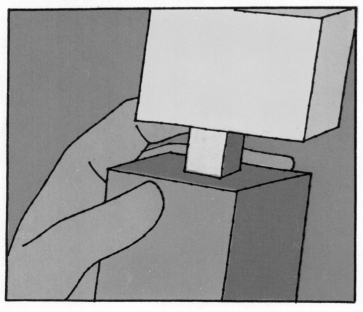

Glue the other end of the neck to the middle of the top edge of the body.

Now stick the arms and legs on. Glue two boxes to the legs at right angles for the feet. Decorate the robot with a black felt-tip pen.

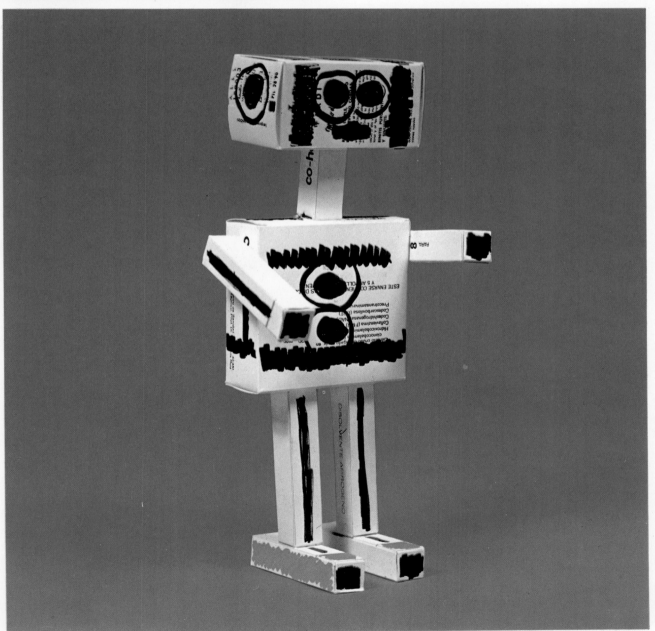

MATERIALS:

- Thick black card
- Thin red card
- Thin string
- Needle
- Scissors

UPRIGHT CONSTRUCTION

Cut a strip of black card 17½in. by 2in.

Fold as shown below.

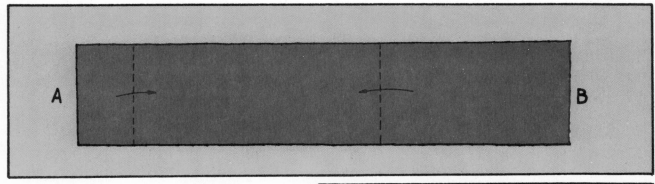

Glue A to B to make the support for the upright.

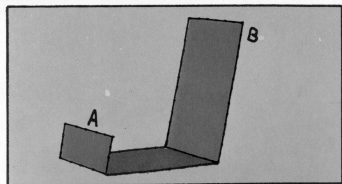

Cut three strips the same width but slightly different lengths out of red card.
Make each one into a ring by gluing the ends together.

Thread a needle with thin string.
Pull the needle through the top of
the support.
Make a knot in the end of the
string.

Thread the string through each
ring, starting with the largest
and finishing with the smallest.
Tie a knot at the end of the string.

Stand the model on a table. The
rings will bend in different direc-
tions if you touch them gently.

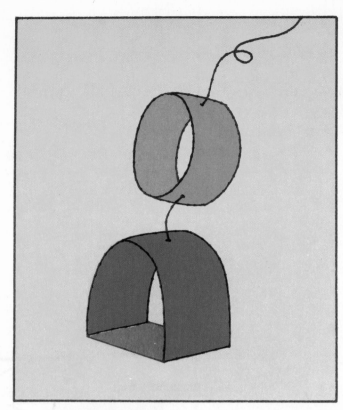

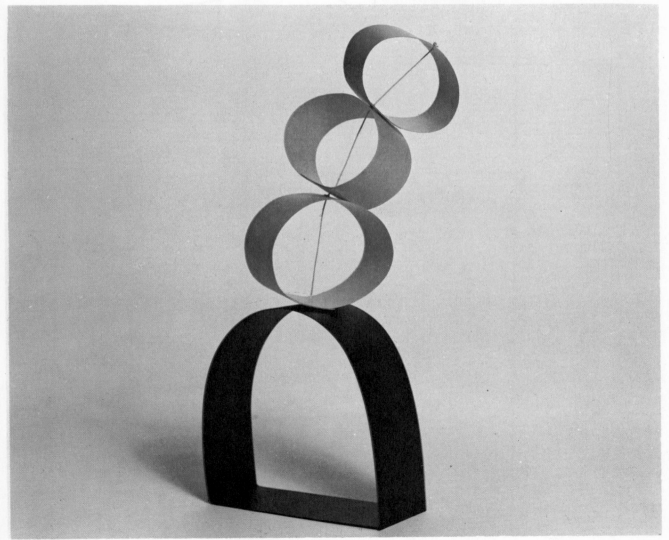

HORSE

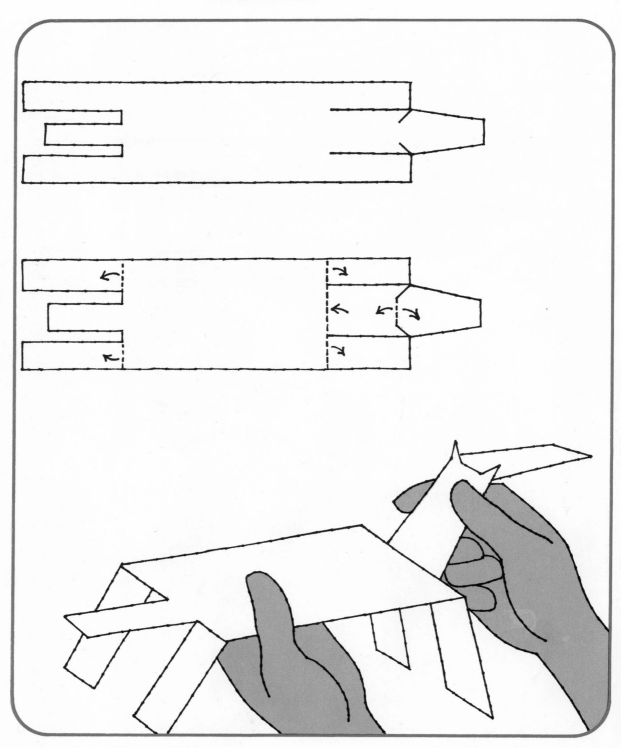

Cut a rectangle 13in. by 3in. out of white card. Draw the shape shown in the diagram. Cut it out. Fold along the dotted lines, following the direction of the arrows.

Fill in the face, neck, feet and tail with a mauve felt-tip pen.

MATERIALS:
● White card
● Ruler
● Pencil
● Scissors
● Mauve felt-tip
   pen

GIRAFFE

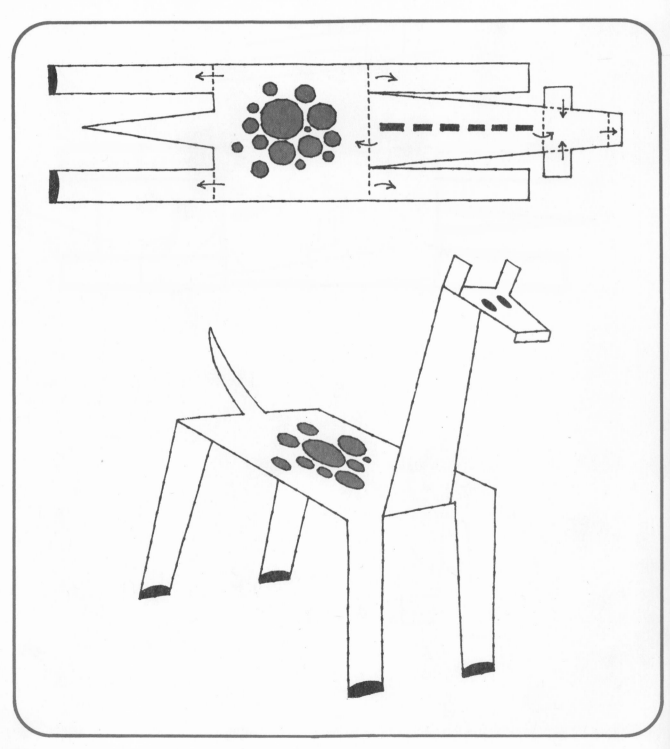

Cut a rectangle 15½in. by 3in. out of white card.

Draw the shape shown in the diagram. Cut it out.

Decorate with a mauve felt-tip pen.

Fold along the dotted lines, following the direction of the arrows.

TIGER

Cut a rectangle 12½in. by 3in. out of white card.
Draw the tiger and cut it out.

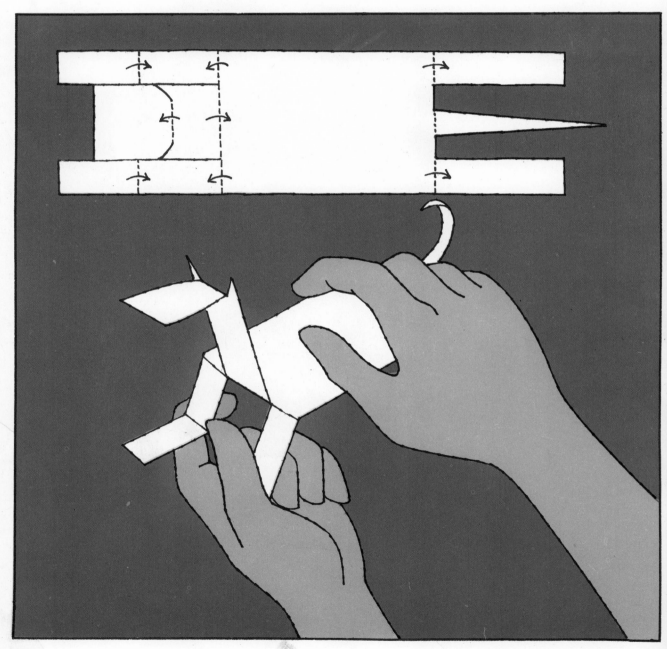

Fill in the tail, body, face and paws with a mauve felt-tip pen.

Fold the outline along the dotted lines, following the direction of the arrows.

MATERIALS:
- **Pink card**
- **Ruler**
- **Pencil**
- **Scissors**
- **Coloured felt-tip pens**

BOOK MARKER

Cut out a rectangle of pink card.

Make the drawing shown in pencil.

Join HP through the middle of FE.

The distance DE is equal to HE.

BC is equal to DE.

PO is equal to PA.

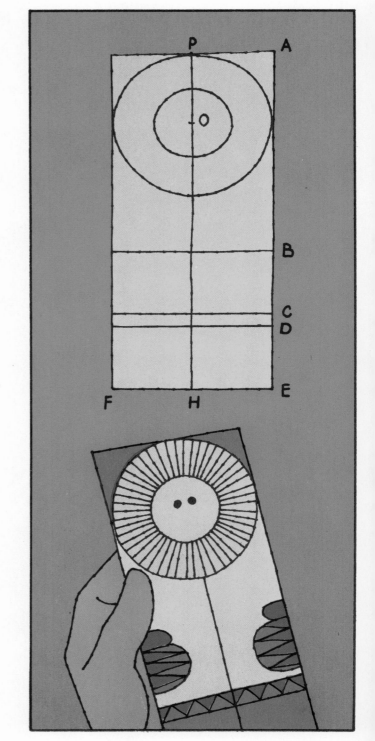

Go over some of the pencil lines in black felt-tip pen as shown in the bottom drawing.

Rub out the pencil marks that are left.

Decorate the marker with coloured felt-tip pens as shown in the picture opposite.

MATERIALS:

- Red card
- Scissors
- Compasses
- Green cellophane
- Needle
- Thin string
- Glue

SUN GLASSES

Draw four equal circles on the red card.

Draw another circle inside each of these as shown in the drawing. Cut round the circles to make four rings.

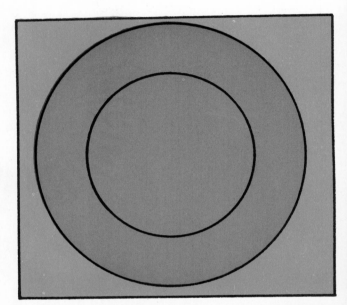

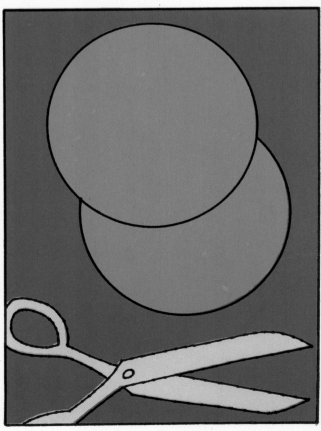

Cut two circles out of green cellophane the same size as the large circles.

Cut a piece like this out of red card.
Fold along the dotted line.

Cut out two strips of red card.

Glue all the parts together as shown in the drawing. Thread some thin string through the ends of the sides of the glasses to fit them on.

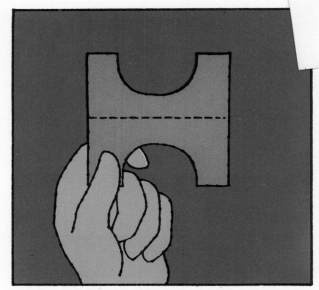

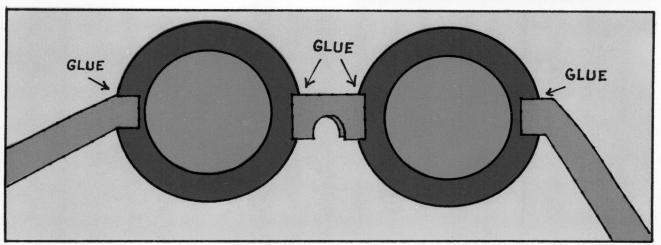

GLUE

GLUE

GLUE

LAMP

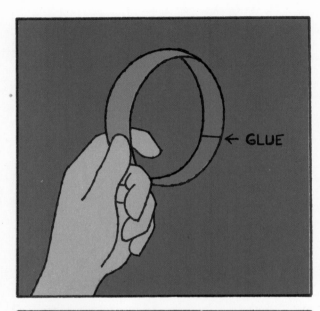

Cut out a strip of green card $17\frac{1}{2}$in. long by $1\frac{3}{4}$in. wide.
Glue the two ends to form a ring. Make another ring the same size in grey.

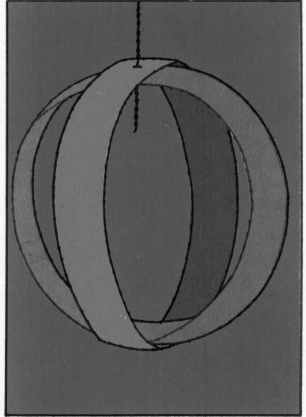

Put one ring inside the other in an upright position. Make a hole at the top where the rings meet. Thread a piece of string about 42in. long through the hole, and tie a knot at the end. Make another knot in the string $3\frac{1}{2}$in. above the top of the rings.

Cut out another two strips of card, one green and one grey, the same width as the first two and about 33in. long. Stick the ends together.

Perforate the new rings and thread the string through, knotting it above the lamp.

MATERIALS:
- Green and white card
- Orange paper
- Two black buttons
- Black cotton
- Sticky tape
- Red felt
- Scissors and glue

BIRD

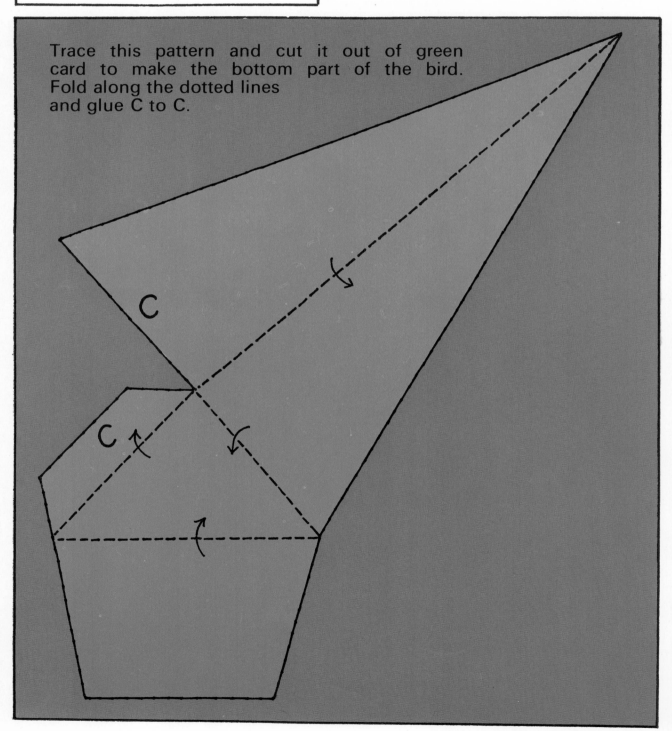

Trace this pattern and cut it out of green card to make the bottom part of the bird. Fold along the dotted lines and glue C to C.

C

C

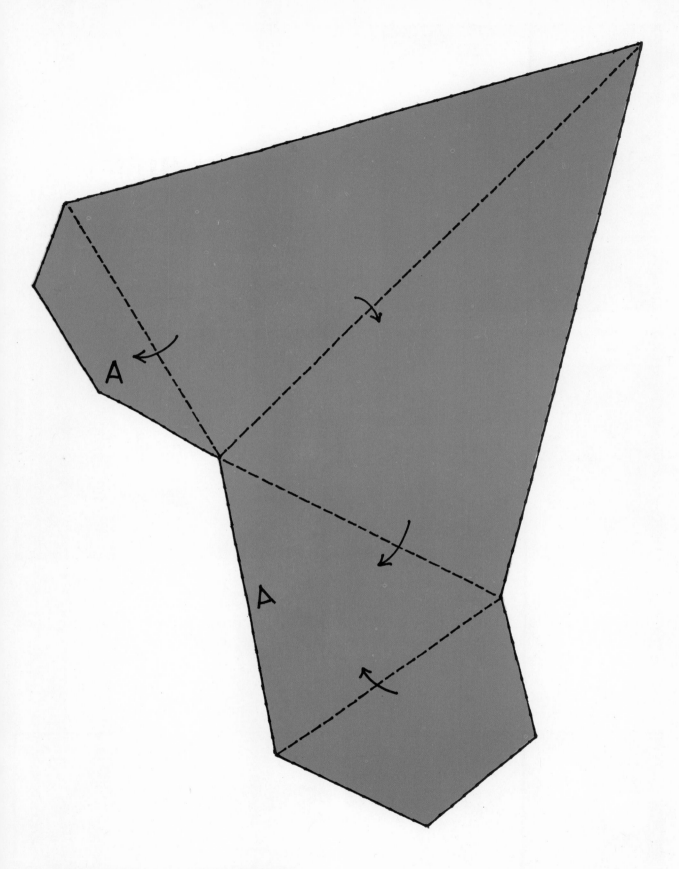

Cut this pattern out of green card.

Fold along the dotted lines, following the direction of the arrows. Glue A to A.

This makes the top part of the bird.

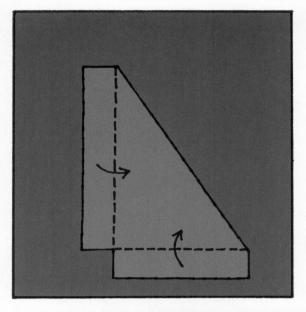

Cut a piece like this out of green card. Fold along the dotted lines and glue one flap on to side C of the top part of the bird, and the other flap on to side B. Cut two circles out of the side triangles.

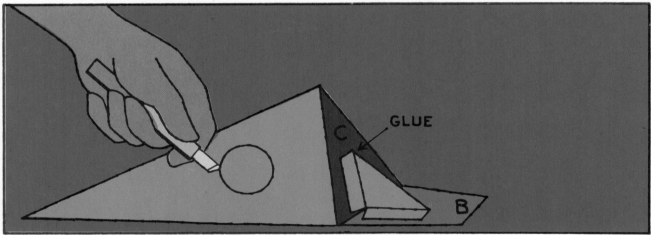

GLUE

Thread the buttons on to a piece of black cotton and stick the ends of the cotton inside the top edge of the eyes with sticky tape.

Cut two rectangles out of white card and glue the ends either side of the eyes, on the inside of the head, to hold the button eyes in place.

Glue B to B.

Cut a tongue out of red felt and glue it on the inside of the mouth.

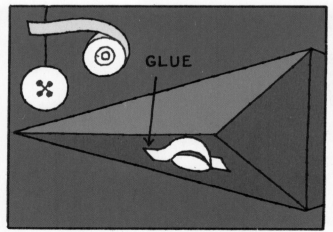

GLUE

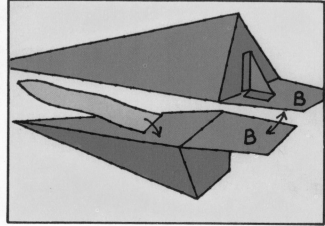

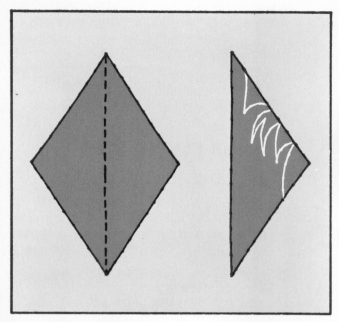

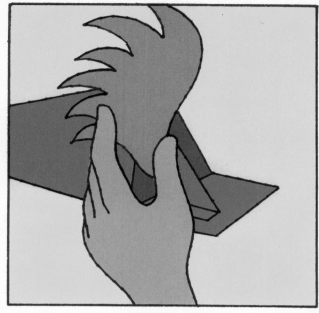

Cut a piece like this out of red felt. Fold along the dotted line and cut round the white lines to make the crest. Make a slit at the bottom of the fold, slot over the support and glue.

Cover the top and bottom of the beak with orange paper.

MOBILE

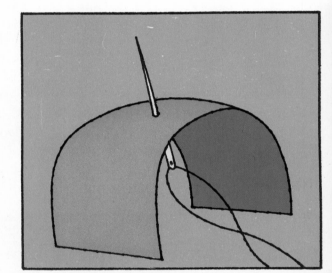

Cut a rectangle out of pink card and bend it into a semicircle to make the support for the mobile. Thread it on to a piece of thin string and knot the end.

Cut four strips the same width but of different lengths out of pink card. Glue the ends of each to make four circles.

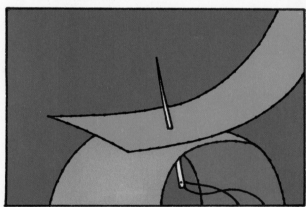

Thread one end of the longest strip on to the string.

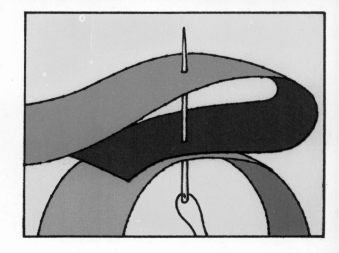

Now fold the strip to the left and push the needle through it again. Continue threading the strip on to the string, folding it right and left as you go, until you come to the end.

Thread on the large pink circle, then the middle strip, and so on.

PAGODA

Cut eight strips 7½in. by 2in. out of black card. Cut four more in orange and twelve in grey.

Glue two pieces of grey card and one black together to make a triangle. Make six of these altogether.

Make two more triangles by gluing two orange and one black card together. In all the pieces except one make a cut 2½in. from either end along the bottom edge of the three sides.

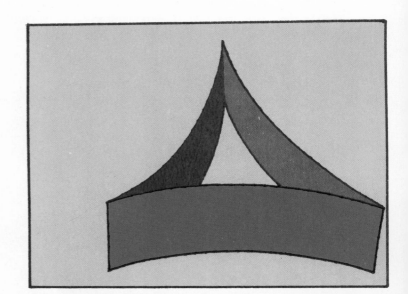

Slot the triangles together like this.

Stand the pagoda on a small triangle, made from two grey strips and one black 5in. by 2in.

The cuts should be made 1½in. from the ends, along the top edge.

MATERIALS:
- Paper
- Black and pink card
- Scissors
- Pencil
- Stapler

HAT

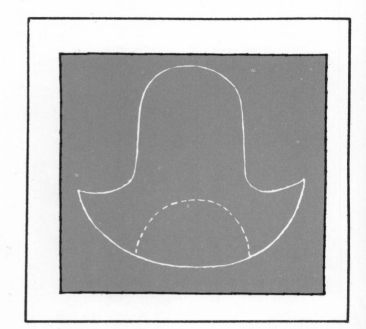

Draw the front and back sections of the hat on paper. The front has a hole cut out at the bottom.

Try these on until they fit your head. Cut them out of black card.

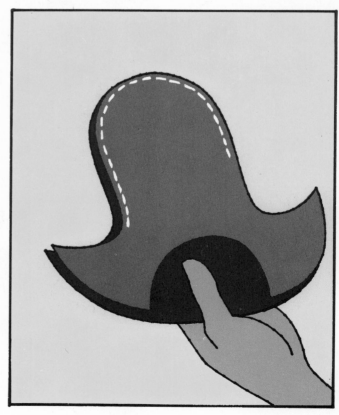

Staple the cards together.

Cut some very narrow strips out of pink card. Join them together at one end. Curl the free ends by pulling them across the edge of a ruler. Staple the flowers to the front of the hat.

MATERIALS:
- Cardboard
- Scissors
- White tissue paper
- Pencil and paper
- Coloured felt-tip pens
- Ribbon

MASK

Trace this drawing, which is half the mask, on a piece of white tissue paper.

Then trace it on to a piece of thick paper folded in half.

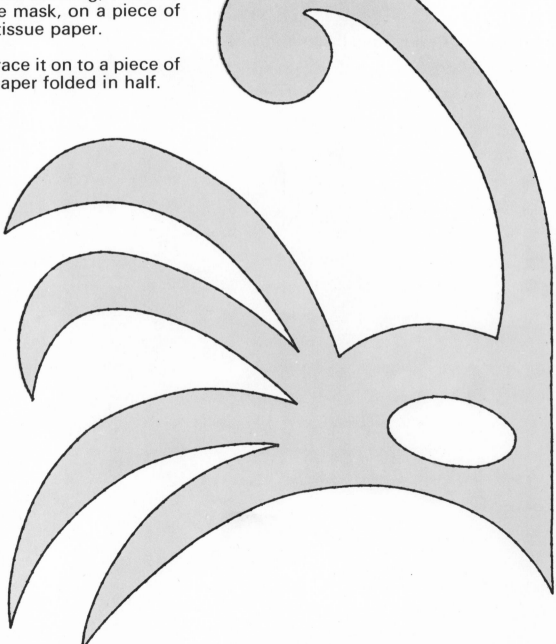

Cut out through both thicknesses.
Open the paper out. You now have the complete pattern for the mask.

Place the pattern on cardboard and draw round the edge in pencil.
Cut it out. Decorate the mask with felt-tip pens.

Tie a ribbon both sides and fasten the mask at the back of your head with a bow.

PICTURE FRAME

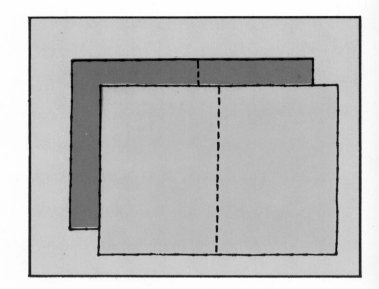

The size of the picture frame will depend on the size of the pictures you want to frame. The one shown is postcard size.

Cut a rectangle 12½in. by 9in., out of green card, and another in cream the same size.

Glue them together.

Cut another rectangle the same size out of black card.
Use a pencil and ruler to mark these lines on it. Cut out the spaces shown in white.
Glue the black card on to the cream one, leaving the corner strips unglued.

Slip the corners of the pictures under these strips. Fold the picture frame in half.

MATERIALS:

- Rectangular box
- White card
- Compasses, ruler and pencil
- Felt-tip pens
- Scissors
- Glue
- Black powder paint

MONEY BOX

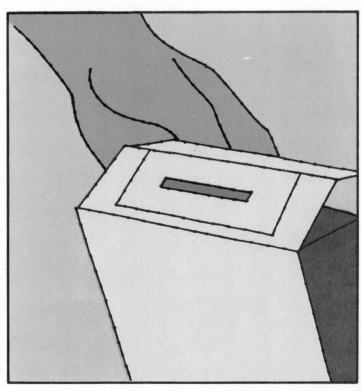

Paint the sides of the box black.

Cut a narrow slit in the lid, and draw round it in black.

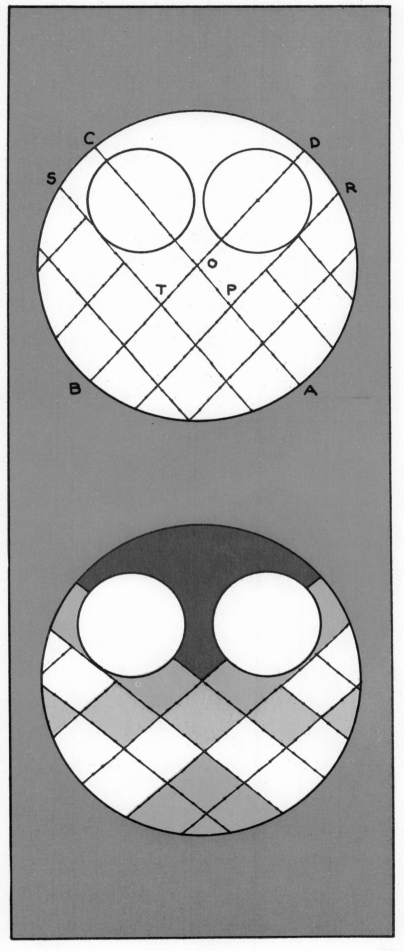

Cut a circle out of white card, making the diameter about 1½in. longer than the height of the box. Join C to A and D to B at right angles.

Divide OA and OB into three equal parts and mark with a dot.

Draw several lines parallel to CA and DB so that they go through the dots.

Place the point of the compasses in the centre of CO and DO and draw two circles.

Divide PR and TS into three equal parts and draw more lines parallel to the two diameters.

These lines will make the squares shown in the drawing.

Now fill in the spaces with felt-tip pens, following this pattern.

Rub out the pencil lines.

Colour the middle of the owl's eyes with a felt-tip pen.

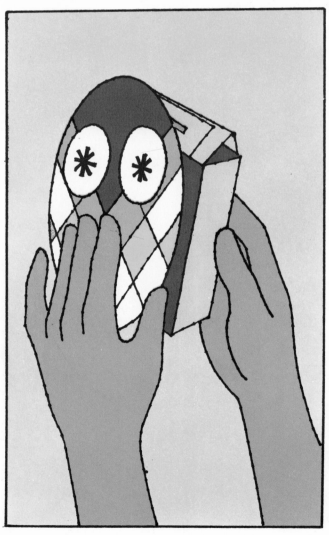

Glue the circle on to the box.

CHICKEN

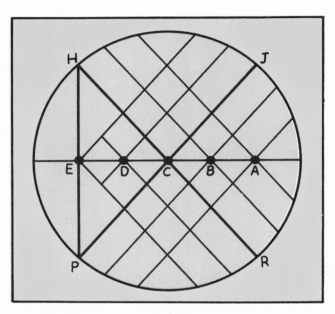

Draw a circle with a radius of $4\frac{1}{2}$in. on blue card. Cut it out. Draw a diameter and divide it into six equal parts. Draw the line PH.

Draw the diameters PJ and HR. Now draw the parallel lines that pass through the points E, D, B, A.

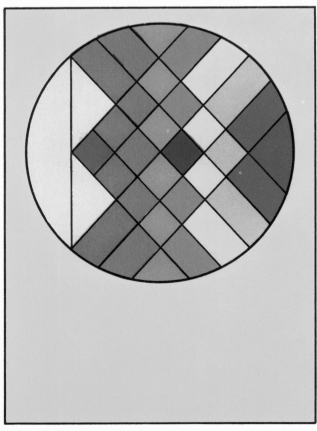

Fill in the squares with felt-tip pens.

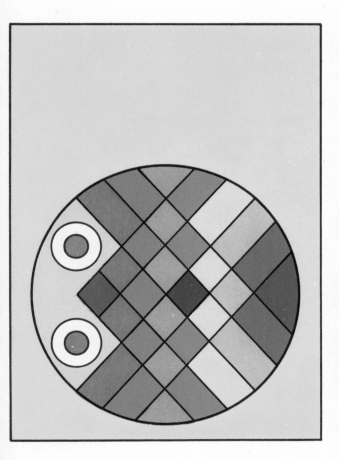

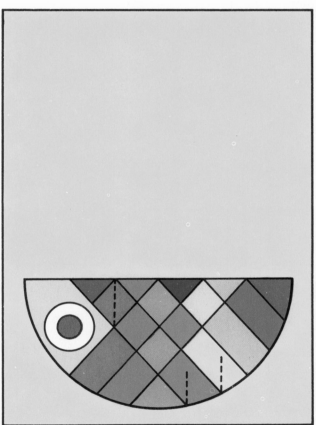

Draw the eyes and fill in the space round them.

Fold the circle in half along the first diameter you drew and make cuts along the dotted lines.

This is the chicken's body.

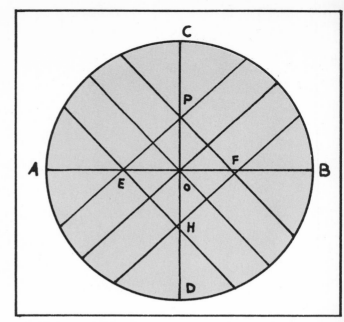

Cut a circle with a radius of 3in. out of blue card.

Draw the diameter AB and divide it as shown in the drawing. Draw the diameter DC at right angles to the first one. Mark off the distance OF along OC and OD to find P and H. Draw a line through E and P and another through H and F. Draw two more lines parallel to each.

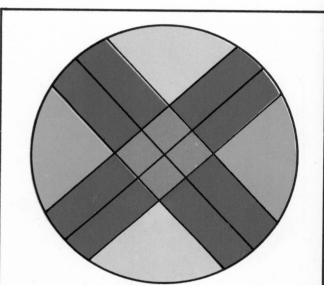

Fill in the squares with felt-tip pens.

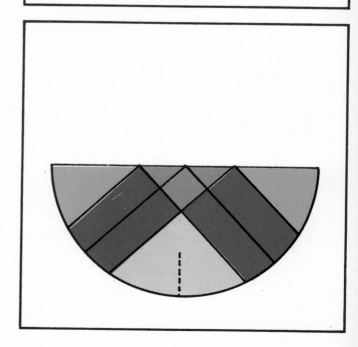

Fold the circle along the first diameter and cut along the dotted line.

Cut another circle with a radius of 1½in. out of black card.

Fold in half and cut along the short dotted line.

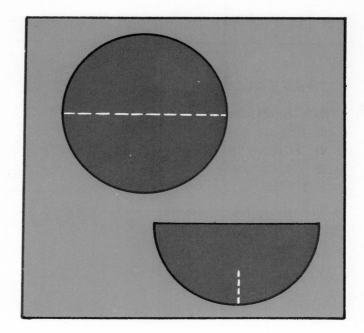

Slot the three pieces together to finish the model.

MATERIALS:

- Cardboard
- Ruler and Pencil
- Scissors
- Thick felt-tip pens

HOUSE

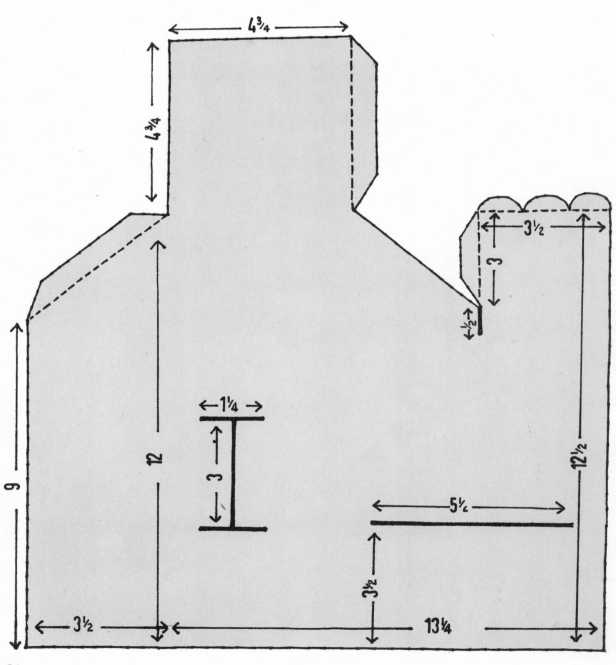

Cut out a piece of cardboard 17in. by 17in. Draw this pattern on it, following the sizes as shown. Cut it out and then cut along the thick black lines shown in the diagram.

Decorate the pattern with felt-tip pens. You can see one way of decorating the shutters (C), and awning (T) and the fence of the little garden (V). You can decorate the house differently. Space T is decorated on the back.

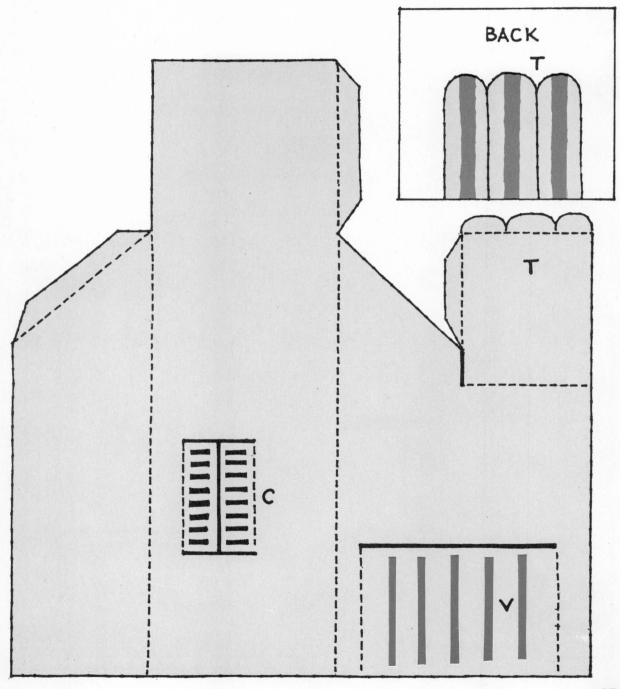

Fold the cardboard along the dotted lines, following the direction of the arrows.

Now glue A to B, C to D, and E to F to make the house.

You can make other kinds of houses and put them together to make a village.

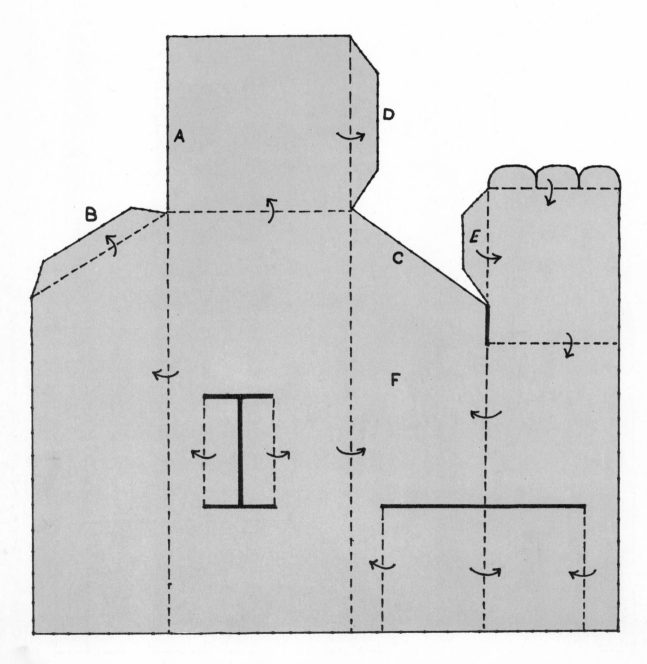

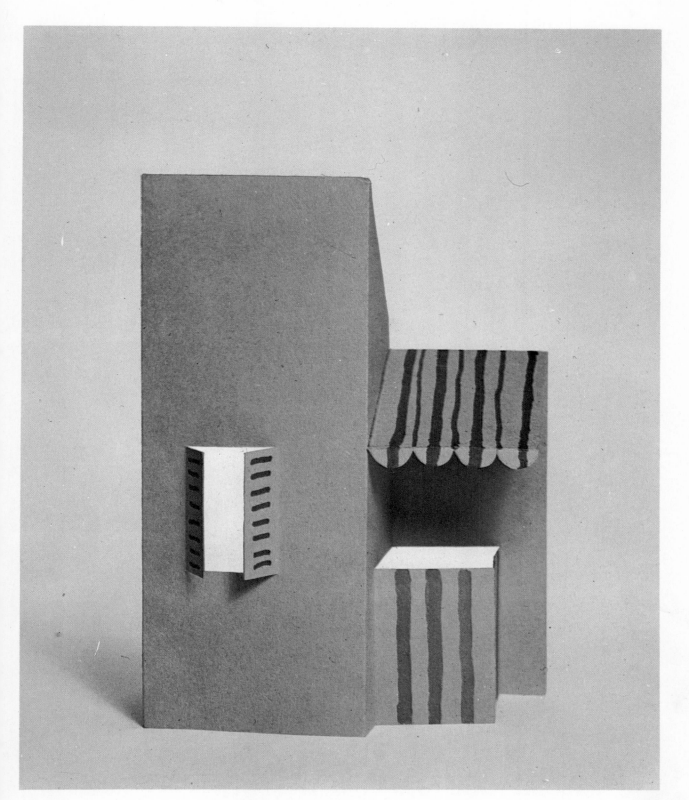

STAR

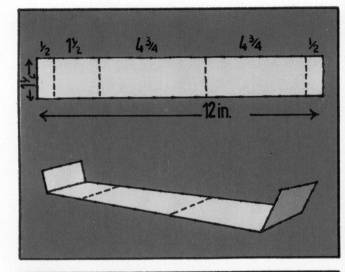

Cut four strips of pink card 12in. by 1½in. and another four the same in orange card.

Fold each strip ½in. from both ends, then make another fold 1½in. from one end fold. Fold again half way along the remaining part of the strip.

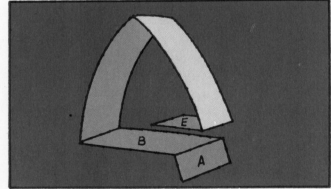

Glue E to B. You now have eight triangles which have a flap A.

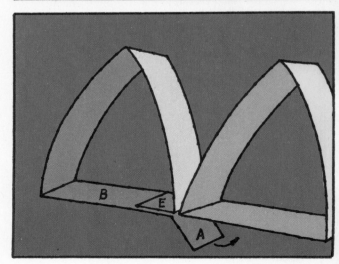

Alternate the colours and glue each surface A underneath B. Finish the star by joining the last flap underneath the first triangle.

SIMPLE CARD RELIEF

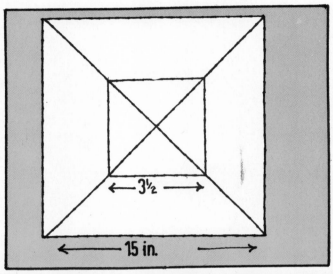

Cut out a piece of white card 15in. square. Draw the diagonals and then another square 3½in. by 3½in.

Cut three strips of white card 6½in. by 1in.

Leave a ¼in. margin at either end of each strip and fold at 1in. intervals.

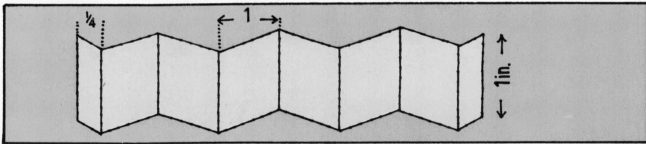

Stick margins at the top and bottom of the middle square, keeping the strips the same distance apart.

Finish the relief by filling in some of the pleats with a black felt-tip pen.

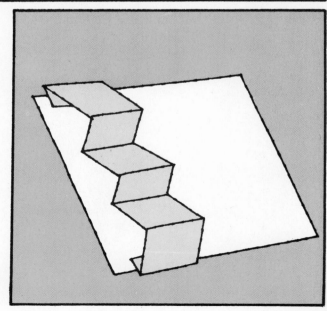

TOWER

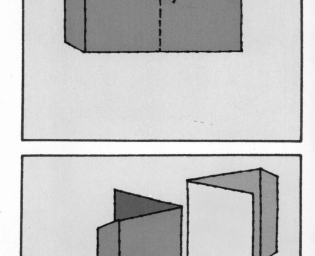

Cut eight strips 3½in. by 2½in. out of red card and eight out of yellow card.

Make a flap down one edge of four red and four yellow strips.

Fold all the strips in half.

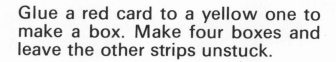

Glue a red card to a yellow one to make a box. Make four boxes and leave the other strips unstuck.

Make a cut in the centre of every top and bottom edge, except on the last box which you only cut at the top.

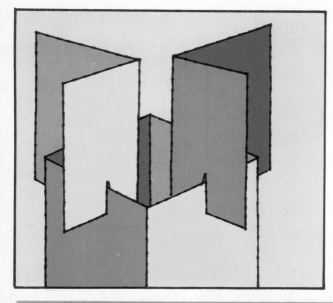

Use the last box as the base of the tower and slot the separate strips and the boxes on to each other alternately to build the tower.

MATERIALS:
- Orange and green card
- Ruler
- Glue
- Scissors
- Pencil

Cut a strip 13½in. by 2in. out of orange card. Glue the ends together to make a circle.

Cut another strip 20in. by 2in. out of green card, and glue the ends to make a 4in. square.

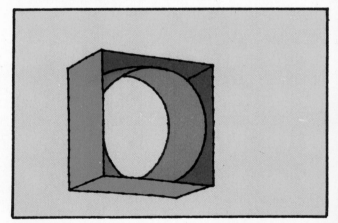

Put the orange ring inside the green square and glue where they join. Cut another strip of orange card 23in. by 2in. Glue the ends and make a 5¼in. square. Put the first circle and square inside this new orange square. Remember that the corners of the green square should touch the outside square in the middle of each side. Glue where they touch.

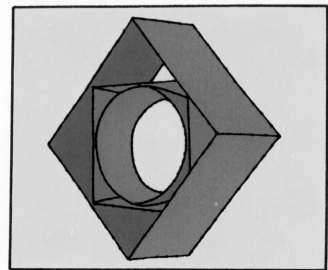

Finally, cut out a green strip 32½in. by 2in. and make a 7½in. square.

Glue this round the outside of the other squares and circles.

RELIEF WITH SEMICYLINDRICAL SHAPES

Cut a 17½in. square out of black card. Cut another square 14in. by 14in. out of white card and a third 12½in. by 12½in. out of blue card.

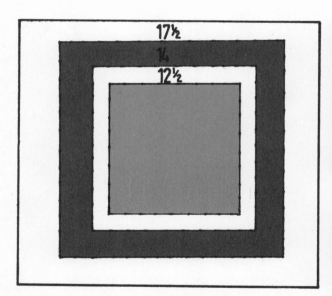

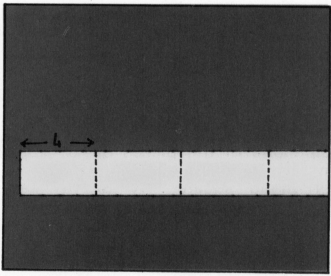

Glue them together, the small one on top and the largest one at the bottom.

Cut strips of metallic card 2in. wide and 4in. long to make twenty-five equal rectangles.

 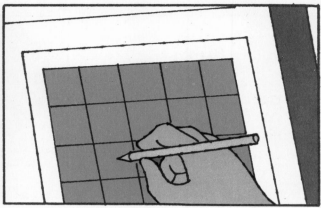

Mark a fold ¼in. from either end of every rectangle.

Draw a 10in. square on the blue square with a faint pencil line.
Divide this into 2in. squares.

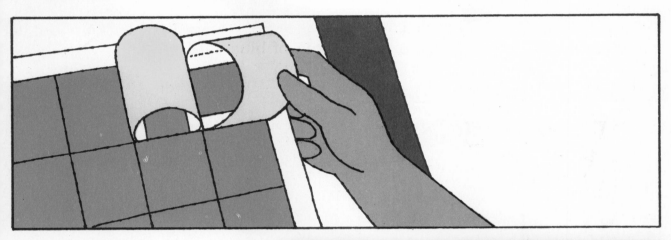

Glue one of the pieces of metallic card on the top left hand square. Try to keep the glue only on the margins otherwise it will spoil the metallic card.

Glue the next piece so that the arc runs in the opposite direction. Alternate the direction of each piece until you have covered all the squares.

You can make up some more patterns and vary the colours of the arcs.

WORM

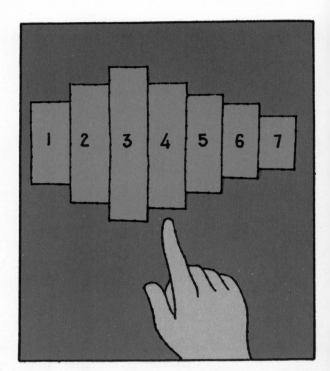

The worm's body is made of seven rings.
Cut seven different rectangles as shown out of green card. Number them.

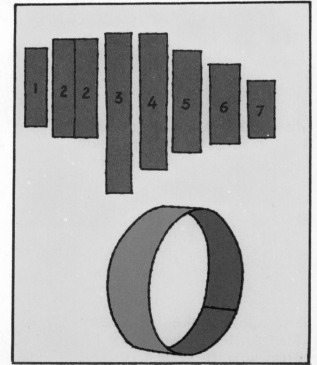

Cut seven strips out of black card the same lengths as the green ones but half as wide.
Number them. Cut a second black strip like number 2.

Glue the ends of each green strip to make rings.

110

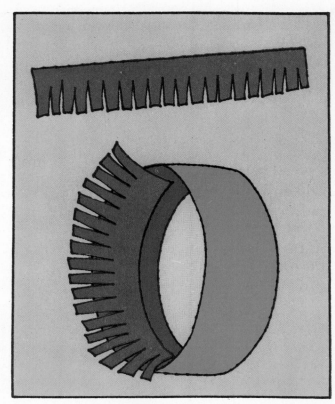

Cut fringes in the black strips.

Glue the bottom of the fringes on the inside edge of each ring. Ring 1 has a fringe at the front, ring 2 at the front and back, and the remaining rings have fringes only at the back.

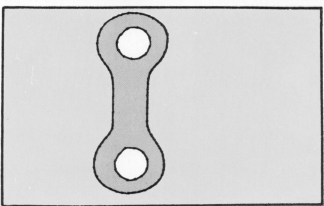

Cut seven shapes like this out of pink card. They are narrower than the rings and each one is about a third as long as the ring it will be stuck on to.
Glue a white circle at each end.

Stick a pink shape on every ring.

Lightly curl all the fringes by pulling them across a sharp edge.

Make a pink fringe and glue it to the last ring underneath the black fringe.

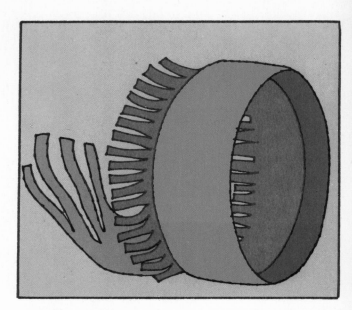

These pieces make the worm's head:
1. A green ring about the same size as the smallest ring for the body.

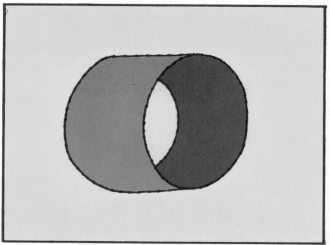

2. A green rectangle. Make two folds in the centre. Cut a fringe along the top and bottom.
Glue the rectangle to the ring.

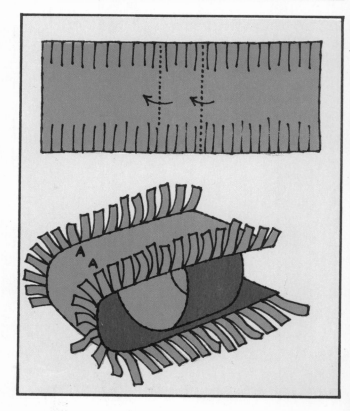

3. Head decoration:

Cut out two white rings.

Cut two rectangles out of red card. Glue the ends.

Make a fringe round the top of each, and make a few cuts round the bottom.

Push each tube through a white ring and glue A on to part A (see left) on the head.

Cut out two black strips and glue them in the shape of a cross on the front of the head.

Sew the green rings together with wool, using oversewing stitches. Tie a long piece of wool underneath the head.
If you pull the worm along the floor it will look as if it is alive.

You can also hang it from the ceiling as a decoration.

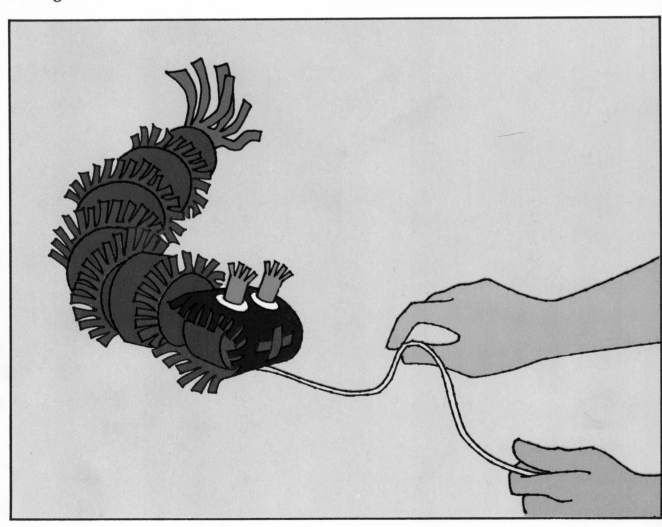

FRAME

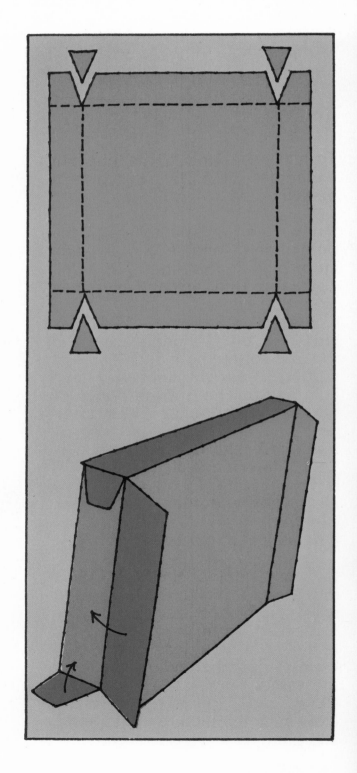

This frame is for a picture 10in. square.

Find the lid of a cardboard box, or make one out of a flat piece of cardboard. The top of the lid should be 15in. square, and the sides 2in. deep.

Cut a 15in. square out of red felt or paper. On the back draw a straight line 2in. in from the four edges, as shown by the dotted lines in the picture.
Cut out four triangles as shown.

Glue the felt or paper round the outside of the lid.

116

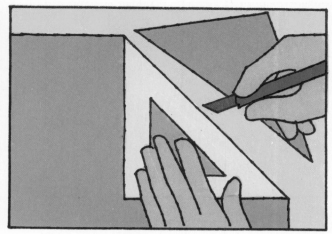

To make the inner frame, cut four rectangles 10in. by 3in. out of metallic card.

Draw four lines parallel to the right hand long edge of each strip, placing the lines $\frac{1}{2}$in., $\frac{3}{4}$in., $1\frac{1}{4}$in. and $1\frac{1}{2}$in. respectively away from that edge.

Now cut off a triangle from the top and bottom right hand corners, cutting across the lines you have just drawn. The outside edges of the triangles should be $1\frac{1}{4}$in. long.

Fold along the four parallel lines. Tuck the outside flap, marked A in the picture, in so that it lies flat on the wide part of the strip. Glue A down.
Do this on all four strips.

Fit these sides of the inner frame together to make a square and stick them on the top of the cardboard lid in the middle.
Make sure you leave an equal amount of red showing all round the frame.

Now stick the picture in the frame and hang on the wall.

MATERIALS:

- Silver and gold metallic card or paper
- Different coloured card
- Scissors
- Glue
- Paper clips
- Pencil

KNIGHT'S HELME

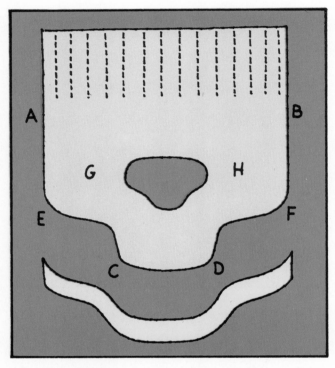

Draw this pattern on silver metallic card. AB should measure the same as the circumference of your head. CD will be about the same as the width of your face.
Cut round the black outline. Cut along the dotted lines and cut out the area shaded black in the picture. The hole should be about 5in. deep.

Cut out a strip of gold coloured metallic card in the same shape as ECDF. Stick the strip along the bottom edge of the silver card.

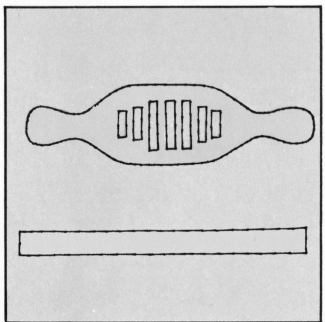

Cut this shape out of shiny silver card. It should be slightly longer than GH. Cut out the strips marked in red to form the visor.

Cut a strip as long as AB out of gold card. Glue this below the cuts you made in the top of the helmet.

118

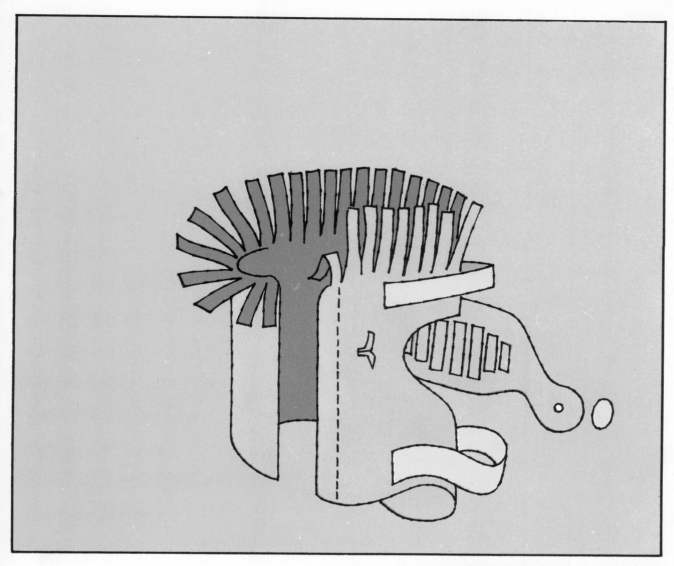

Cut two small circles out of gold card. Put the visor across the hole in the helmet and hold it in place with paper clips, which you push through from the inside of the helmet, then through the visor and the gold circles.

Bend the helmet into a cylinder and glue the edges.

Cut rectangles out of different coloured card. Fold them in half lengthwise and draw a feather. Cut out and cut fringes all round the edge.

Curl the fringes round a pencil.

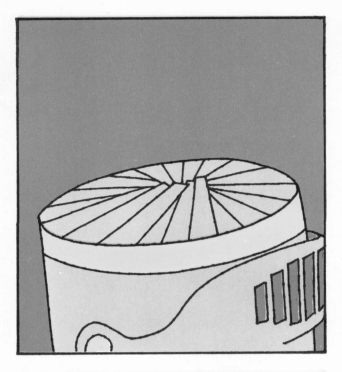

Fold the cuts at the top of the helmet inwards and glue the ends one on top of the other.

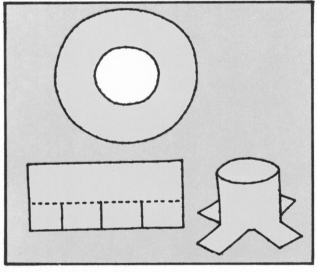

Cut a ring out of gold card to fit round the top edge of the helmet. Stick it down.

Now cut a small rectangle out of gold card. Make three cuts up to the dotted line and fold the flaps out.

Glue the ends of the rectangle together to make a holder for the feathers.

Arrange the feathers in the holder so that they stay in the shape of a tuft.
Finally, glue the flaps of the holder on the top of the helmet.

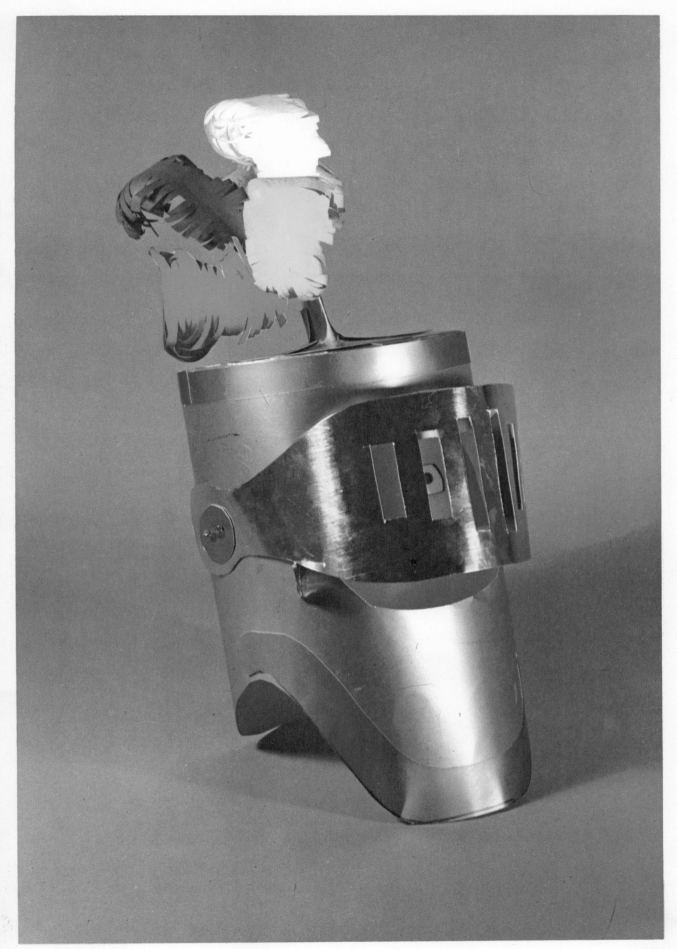

MATERIALS:

● Different
  coloured card
● Scissors
● Glue
● Ruler
● Pencil

OWL

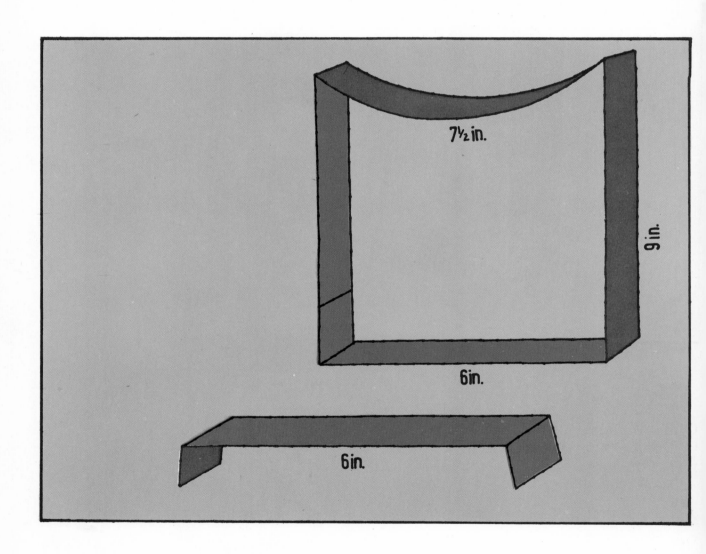

7½ in.

9 in.

6 in.

6 in.

Cut a strip 33in. by 1½in. out of black card. Fold it according to the measurements shown in the picture and glue the ends so that they overlap by about 1½in.

Cut a strip 8in. by 1in. out of black card. Fold down the ends.

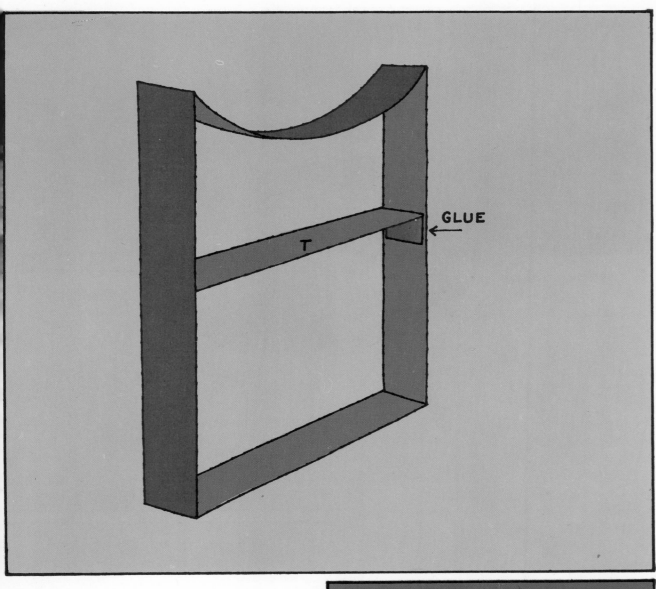

GLUE

T

Glue this strip inside the shape you have just made, about 5in. from the base.

Cut two strips 15in. by 1in. out of blue card. Fold one end of each as shown and curl the other end with scissors. Glue H to H and stick the S flaps in the middle of the strip marked T in the picture above.

Glue a green circle in the middle of each spiral.

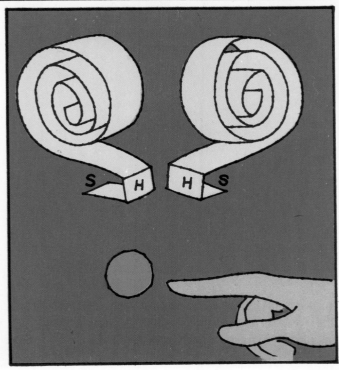

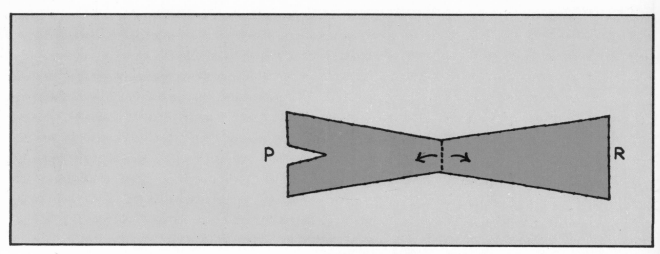

Cut a piece as shown above out of red card to make the owl's beak. Fold it in half.

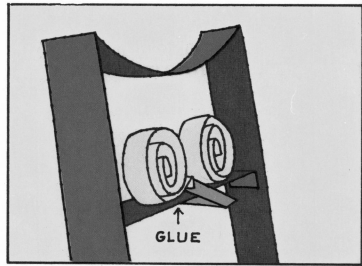

GLUE

Fit end P round the eyes and glue base R underneath strip T. Cut strips like these out of different coloured cards and glue them on the inside of the walls.

Cut two strips of black
card. Fold each one like
this to make the owl's
feet.

Glue the top part of the feet underneath the base. Glue the bottom of the feet
on a rectangle of card to make the owl stand up.

INDIAN MASK

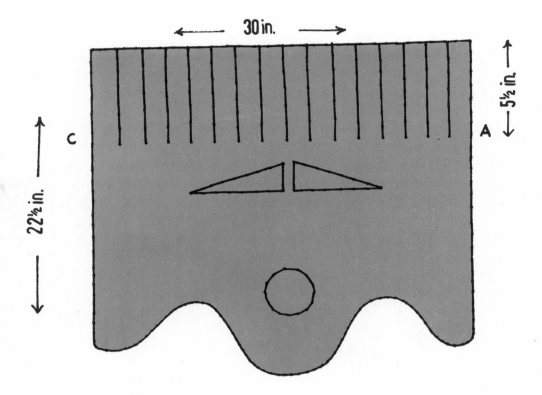

Draw this shape on grey card. Make cuts 5½in. deep along the top. Cut out the triangles and the circle to fit over your eyes and mouth. Keep the triangles you have cut out. Cut a green strip and glue it from C to A.

Put the triangles that you cut out of the mask on a piece of black card and draw round the edge in pencil. Draw a bigger triangle round the first one. Cut round the edge of the two triangles to make an open triangle. Make two open triangles and glue them round the eye holes in the mask.

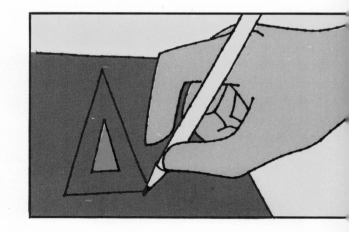

Cut two large triangles like this one out of red card and glue them under the eyes with the top points of the triangles pointing inwards. Cut some green strips and glue them along the inside edges of the red triangles.

Cut out two small black triangles and glue them over the apex of the two red ones, so they point in the same direction as the eye holes.

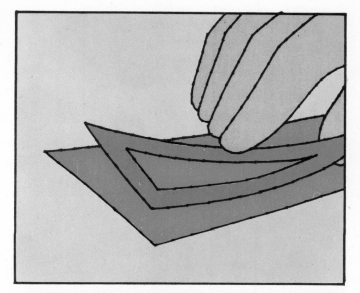

Cut a black strip the same shape as the bottom edge of the mask.

Cut a very fine fringe along the bottom of the strip. Glue the top of the strip to the bottom of the mask on the inside. Curl the fringes round a pencil.

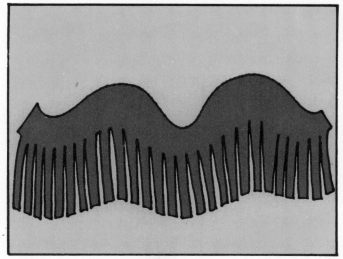

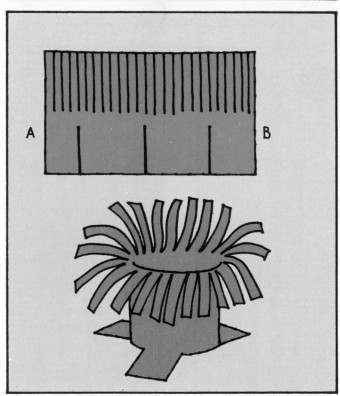

Cut a wide strip out of orange card to fit round the hole for the mouth.
Cut a fringe at the top and make a few cuts along the bottom and fold the flaps out.
Glue A to B.
Push this little tube through the hole in the mask so that it sticks out at the front. Glue the flaps on the back of the mask.

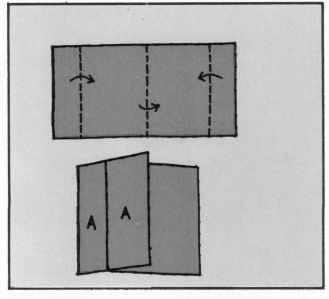

Cut two rectangles out of orange card. Fold along the dotted lines, following the direction of the arrows. Glue the parts A on the mask to make ears.

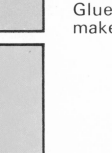

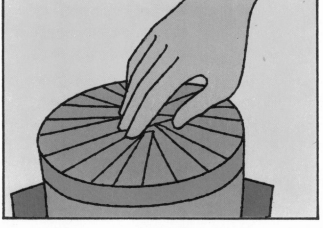

Fold the cuts at the top of the mask inwards, as shown in the drawing. Join the ends in the middle.

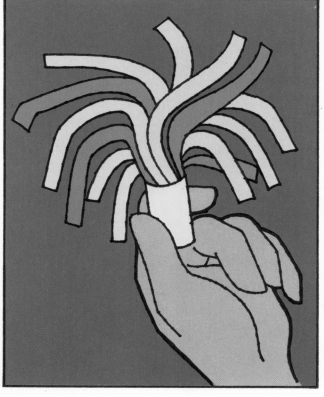

Cut very fine fringes in blue and white card, and roll them up to make two sprays. Wrap a strip of card round the bottom of the sprays and clip to the top of the mask, in the middle. Curl the fringes round a pencil.

AEROPLANE

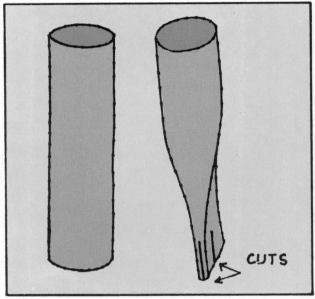

Cut a rectangle 12½in. by 8½in. out of orange card and glue the long edges together to make a tube.

Flatten out one end of the cylinder to make the tail of the plane.

Make 1in. cuts in the middle and on one edge of the flat end.

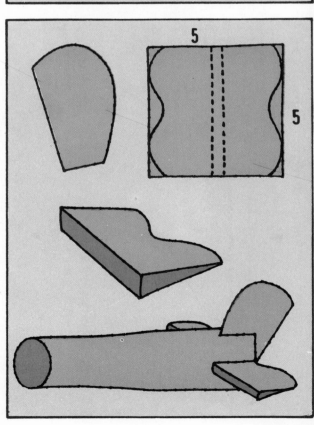

Cut the shape of a butterfly wing out of a piece of orange card 3in. by 2in.

Take a piece of card 5in. square. Fold either side of the centre as shown by the dotted lines in the picture. Cut along the wavy lines on the left and right hand side of the fold lines, and glue these edges together.

Slot the two pieces into the cuts in the tail and glue them to form the rudders.

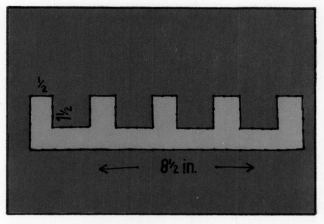

To make the engine, cut this shape out of grey card and wrap it round the open end of the cylinder. Glue the ends of the flaps.

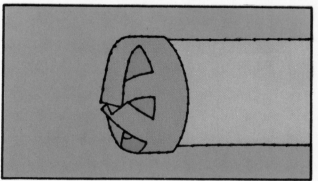

Cut a propeller 5in. long out of yellow card. Pin it in the middle of the engine.

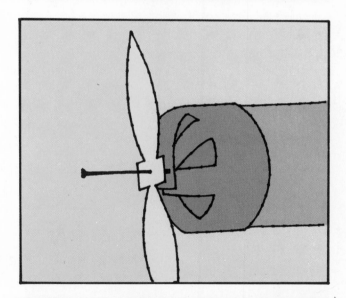

Cut two rectangles 12½in. by 7½in. out of orange card for the wings. Make two folds down the middle, ½in. apart. Glue the edges together and cut off the two corners and the middle of these edges as shown in the picture.
Glue one wing underneath the plane behind the engine.

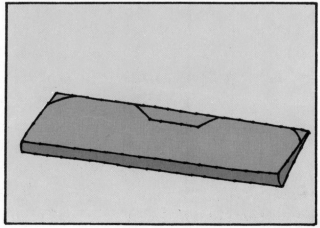

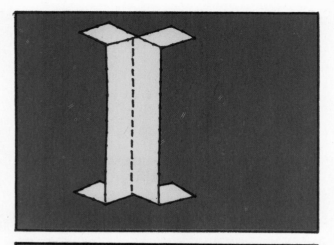

Cut out four yellow strips and make a $\frac{1}{2}$in. cut either end. Fold out the flaps and glue them on the lower wing. Glue the top wing to the top flaps.

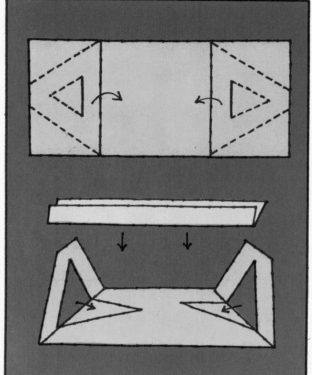

To make the undercarriage, cut out a rectangle 6in. by $2\frac{1}{4}$in. Draw a $2\frac{1}{4}$in. square in the middle and turn the ends into triangles by cutting along the dotted lines shown in the drawing. Fold the triangles so they stand upright and join them at the top with a folded strip of card, like the ones supporting the wings. Glue the undercarriage in the centre of the lower wing.

Cut two circles of 1in. radius out of grey card and another two of $\frac{1}{2}$in. radius out of yellow card. Stick the yellow ones on to the grey ones and join them to the undercarriage with a piece of wire.
Cut out another grey circle, wire it to a yellow strip like the one in the drawing and glue underneath the plane.

Finish the plane by cutting a hole in the cylinder behind the top wing for the cabin. Make a pilot's head to sit in the hole.

THEATRE

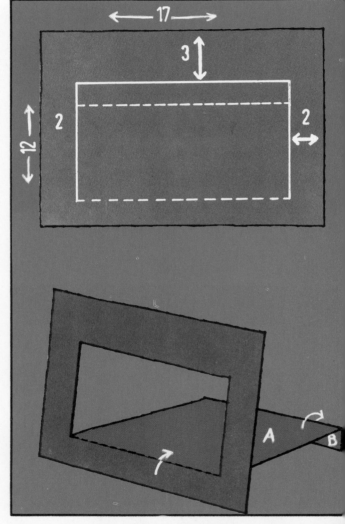

Cut a rectangle 17in. by 12in. out of black card.

Draw three sides of a smaller rectangle 3in., 2in. and 2in. from three sides of the card. Cut along these lines, marked by a solid white line in the diagram.

Fold the card along the dotted lines, following the direction of the arrows.

Surface A will be the stage floor.

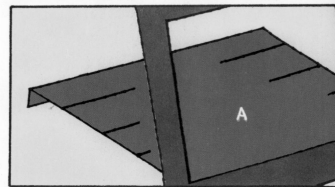

Make three cuts 3in., 2in. and ½in. long respectively on either side of the floor.

Cut a rectangle 17in. by 12in. out of pale blue card to make the back curtain. Glue flap B to the bottom edge of the curtain.

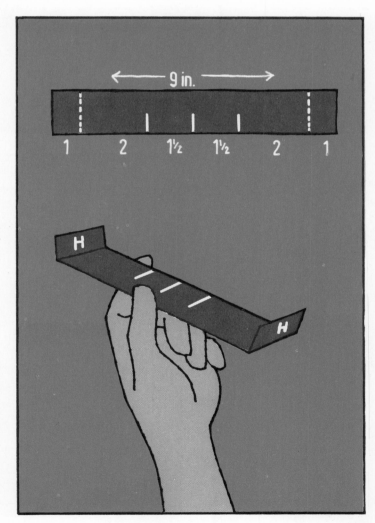

Cut two strips out of black card 9in. by 2in. for joining the top of the curtain and the front of the stage. Make 1in. cuts indicated by the solid white lines in the picture. Fold along the dotted lines.

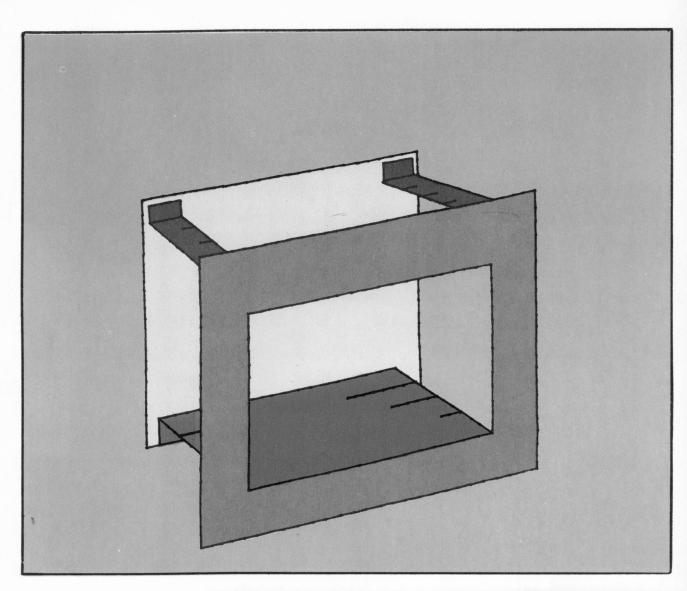

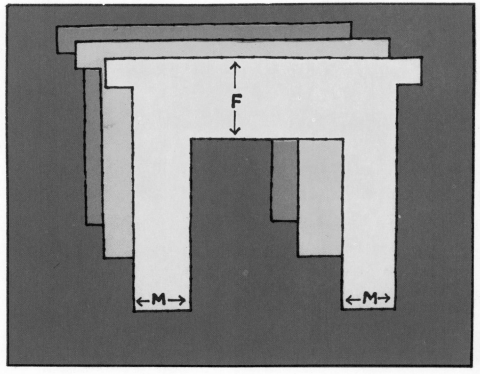

Glue these strips to the curtain and front of the stage at the top.

The wings are made from coloured card.
Distance F will be 3½in. for the first wing, 4in. for the second and 4½in. for the third.

Distance M will be 2in. for the first, 2½in. for the second and 3in. for the third.

Slot the wings into the cuts in the supports and in the side of the floor.

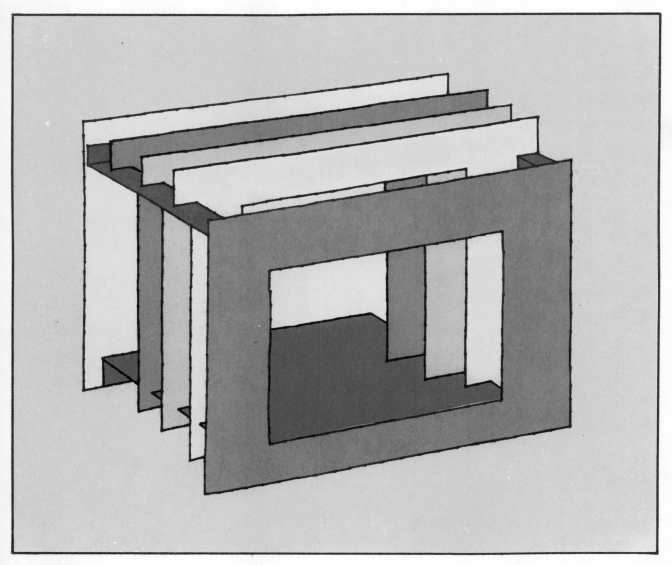

Cut a strip of black card longer than the width of the stage. The strip should be about 1 in. wide.

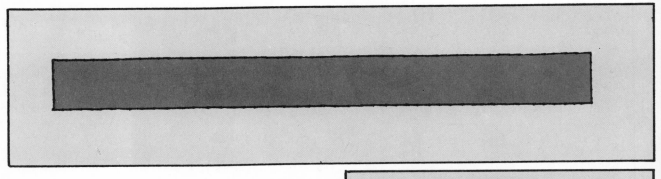

Cut a rectangle 2½ in. by 1 in. out of black card. Fold along the dotted line shown in the picture.

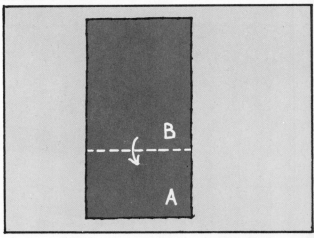

Draw the character on surface B and paint it white.

Glue surface A at one end of the strip.

Slide the strip through the wings and move it about to make the character move about on the stage.

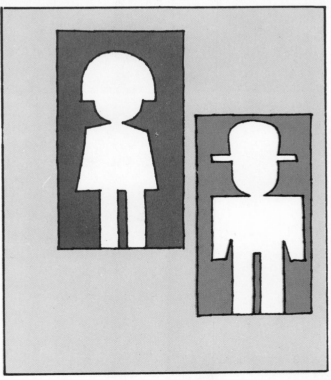

To make the scenery, cut rectangles out of black card.

Draw the scenery you need on the pieces of card.

Make a fold at the bottom of the rectangle to serve as a support.

RELIEF WITH ANGLES AND CYLINDERS

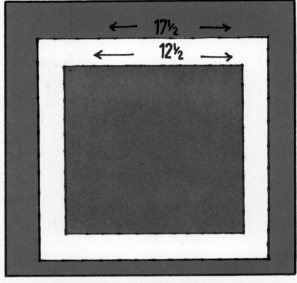

Cut a 17½in. square out of white card. Cut out a 12½in. square and glue it in the middle of the large one.

Lightly draw in a third square, 10in. by 10in., in the middle of the top one. Divide it into 2½in. squares.

Cut a strip 40in. by 2½in. out of red card and another the same size out of metallic card.
Cut each strip into eight rectangles 5in. by 2½in.

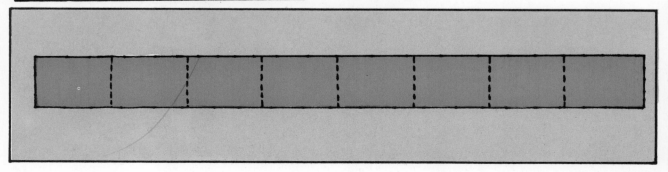

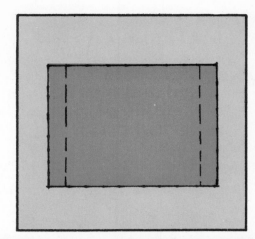

Fold back the short edges to make ½in. flaps.
Glue one of the red rectangles in the top left
hand pencil square like this.

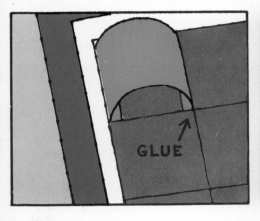  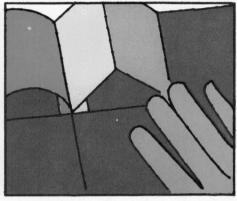

Make a fold across the middle of the metallic rectangles and glue one of them
next to the red one.

Fill up all the squares, alternating the red and metallic pieces across and down.

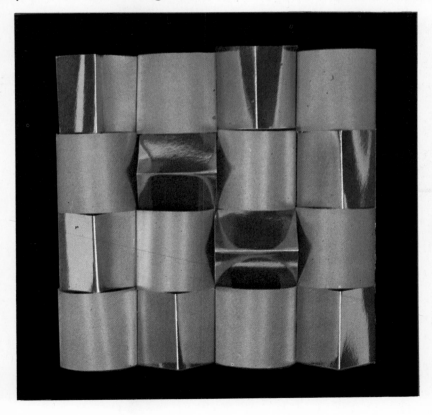

RELIEF IN A CIRCLE

Cut a 12½in. square out of cardboard. Cut a rectangle 14in. by 11½in. out of metallic card.

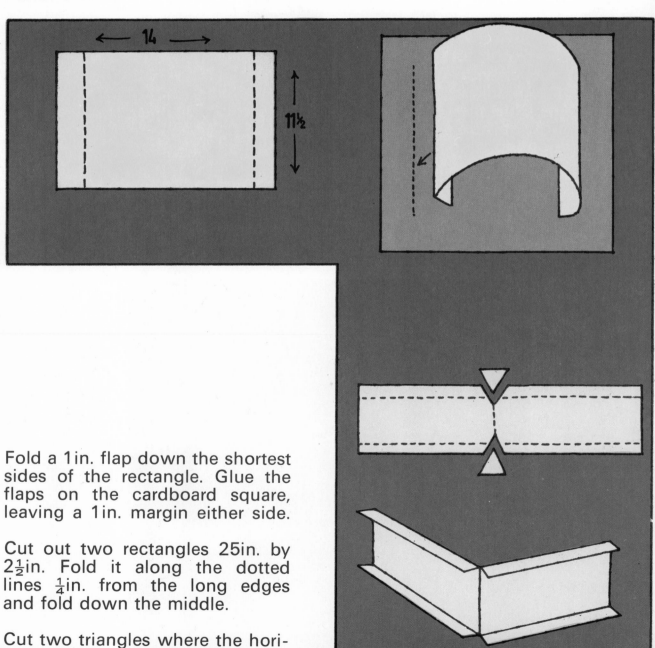

Fold a 1in. flap down the shortest sides of the rectangle. Glue the flaps on the cardboard square, leaving a 1in. margin either side.

Cut out two rectangles 25in. by 2½in. Fold it along the dotted lines ¼in. from the long edges and fold down the middle.

Cut two triangles where the horizontal folds cross the vertical fold.

Glue the two rectangles round the top edges of the square to make a box shape.

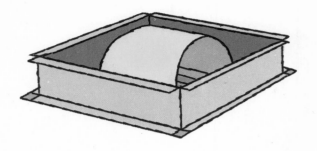

Cut a 12½in. square out of black card. Draw in the two diagonals to find the middle of the square. Draw a circle with a radius of 3¾in. in the middle of the square. Cut it out. Glue the card on the top flaps of the box sides. Finish the work, gluing it on a square of red card measuring 17½in. per side.

MATERIALS:

- Cardboard
- Black and white card
- Metallic card or paper
- Scissors
- Glue
- Compasses, ruler and pencil

RELIEF WITH TWO CIRCLES

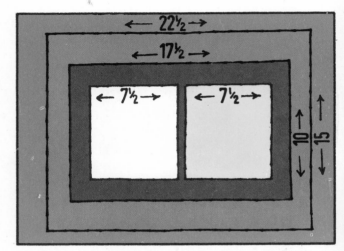

Cut a rectangle 22½in. by 15in. out of cardboard and another 17½in. by 10in. out of black card. Glue the black rectangle on the cardboard leaving a 2½in. margin at the top and the bottom. Cut two 7½in. squares out of white card and another two the same size out of metallic card.

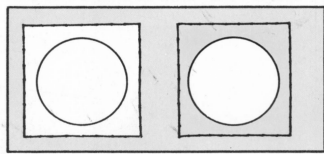

Glue one white square and one metallic square next to each other on the black rectangle, leaving a 1¼in. margin all round.

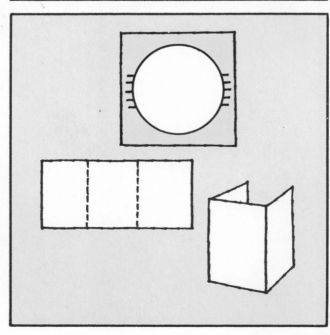

Draw a circle with a 2½in. radius in the centre of the remaining squares. Cut out the circles.

Make five ¼in. cuts either side of the circle about ¾in. apart.

Cut eight rectangles 1½in. by ¾in. out of white card. Fold along the dotted lines. Glue these supports to the corners of the white and metallic squares.

146

Put the white card with the hole in the middle over the solid metallic card, and the metallic over the white. Glue to the top flaps of the supports.

Cut five strips ½in. wide out of metallic card and five out of white card.
One should be 5½in. long, two should be 5in. long, and two 4½in. long.

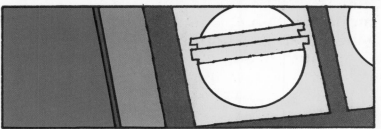

Slot the strips into the cuts in the circles, matching the colours of the strips and circles. Put a spot of glue underneath each join.

RELIEF WITH A RED CIRCLE

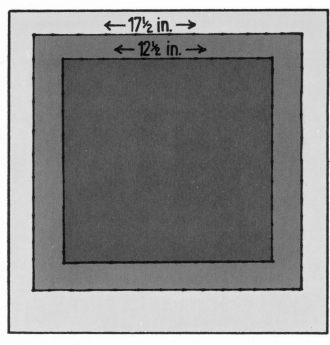

←17½ in.→

←12½ in.→

Cut a 17½in. square out of cardboard. Cut a second square 12½in. by 12½in. out of black card. Glue the black square in the centre of the cardboard square.
There should be a 2½in. margin all the way round the black square.

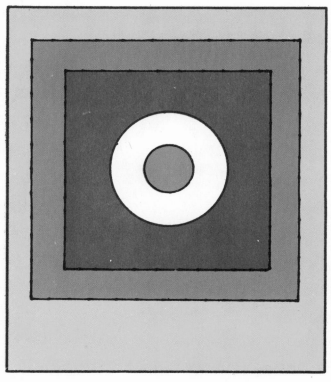

Cut out a circle 5¾in. across out of white card and glue it in the centre of the black square.
Cut another circle 2½in. across out of red card and glue it in the middle of the white circle.

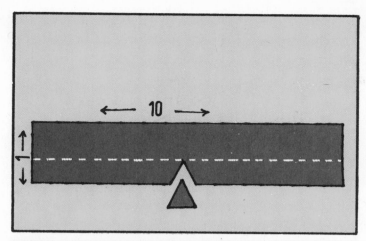

Cut four strips 10in. by 1in. out of black card. Make a fold $\frac{1}{4}$in. in from the bottom edge and cut a small triangle in the centre, so that you can fold the strip at right angles.

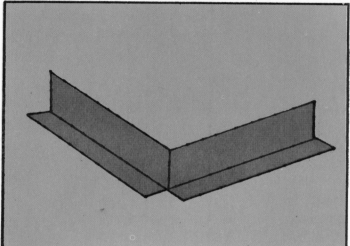

Glue the four strips at the corners of the black square.

Cut a 12½in. square out of white card and cut a circle with a radius of 4in. out of the middle.

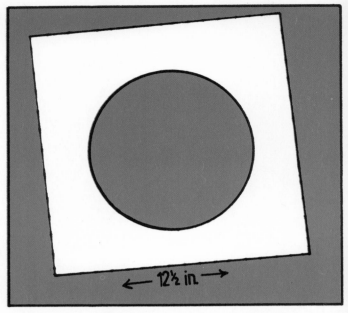

Cut twenty-eight strips ½in. wide out of white card. Cut them in twos, making the first two 8½in. long and gradually making them shorter until you reach the last two, which should both be 4in. long.

Make a ¼in. cut at the top and bottom of each strip as shown in the drawing and fold along the dotted line.

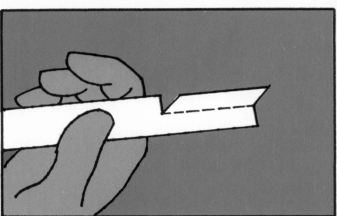

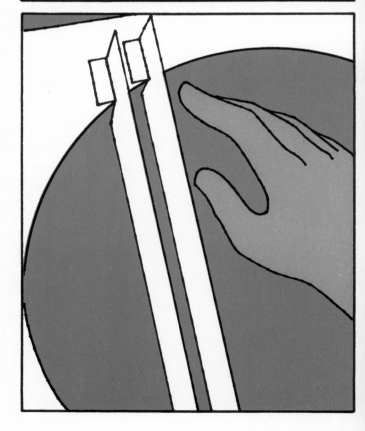

Glue the flaps on the back of the circle, keeping the strips parallel and leaving the same distance between one and the next.

Put the white circle on the supports so that you can see the other circles through the bars.

MATERIALS:

- Cardboard
- Blue card, and gold and silver metallic card or paper
- Scissors
- Glue
- Compasses, ruler and pencil

BLUE RELIEF

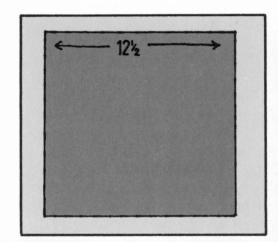

Cut a 12½in. square out of cardboard.
Cut a strip 25in. by 3in. out of silver card.
Cut it into four rectangles, two 7½in. long and two 5in. long.

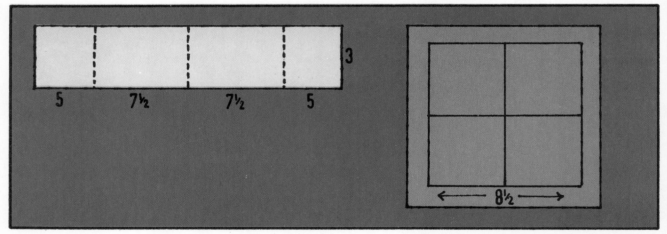

Draw an 8½in. square in the middle of the cardboard square and divide it into four.

Make a fold ¼in. in from the shortest sides of the two small pieces of silver card. Glue them on two of the small squares you have just drawn. They will bend into an arch.

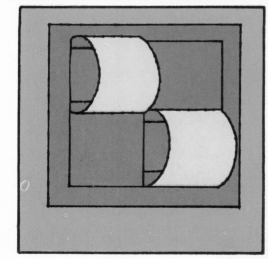

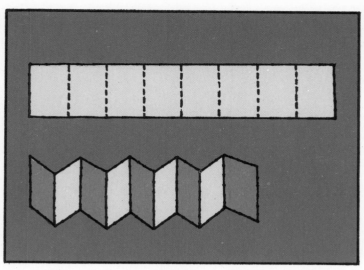

Make a fold $\frac{1}{4}$in. in from the shortest sides of the two remaining pieces of silver card. Draw parallel lines 1 in. apart along the rest of the strip and fold as shown, to make pleats. Glue the pleated strips on the two empty squares.

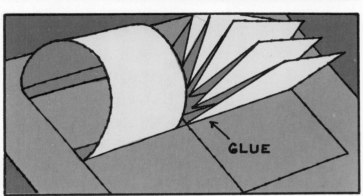

GLUE

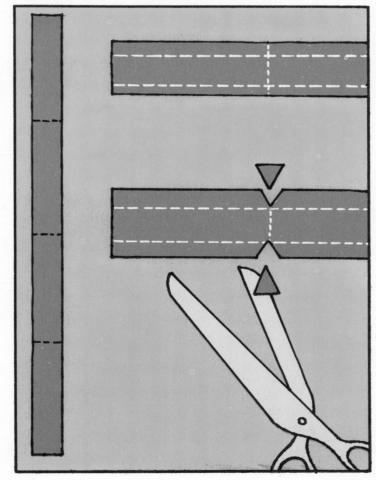

Cut four strips 12$\frac{1}{2}$in. by 3$\frac{1}{2}$in. out of blue card.

Fold along the dotted white lines, $\frac{1}{2}$in. in from the edges, and down the middle.
Cut out two small triangles as shown.

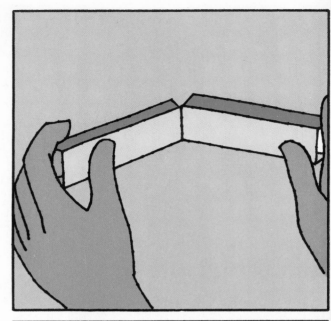

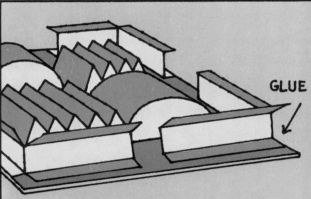

GLUE

Glue the strips on the cardboard square so that the design is boxed in.

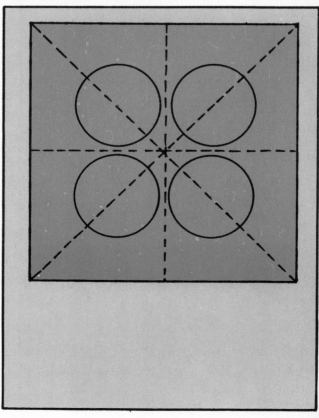

Cut another 12½in. square out of blue card. Mark the diagonals and middle lines on the back. Draw four circles with a radius of 1½in., leaving ½in. between them.
Cut them out.
Glue this card on to the top flaps of the box.
Finally, glue the design in the middle of a 15in. square of metallic card.

RELIEF WITH ANGLES

Cut a 15in. square out of white card.
Cut a 5in. square out of silver card.
Glue the silver square in the middle of the white one.
Cut two rectangles 5in. by 3¾in. out of silver card. Glue them on the white card, above and below the silver square.

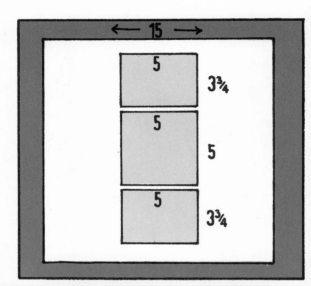

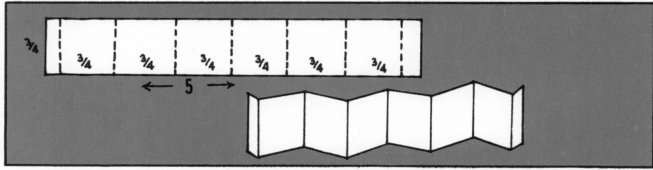

Cut nine strips 5in. by ¾in. out of white card.
Mark fold lines along the strips ¾in. apart, starting ¼in. in from either end.
Fold each strip along these lines as above to make pleats.

Glue three pleated strips on the middle square.

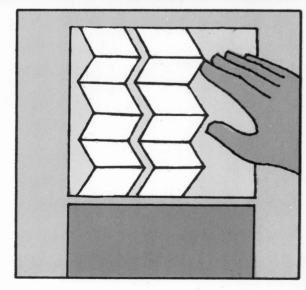

Glue the other strips on the rectangles. Cover some sides of the pleats with a black felt-tip pen.

PICTURE FRAME

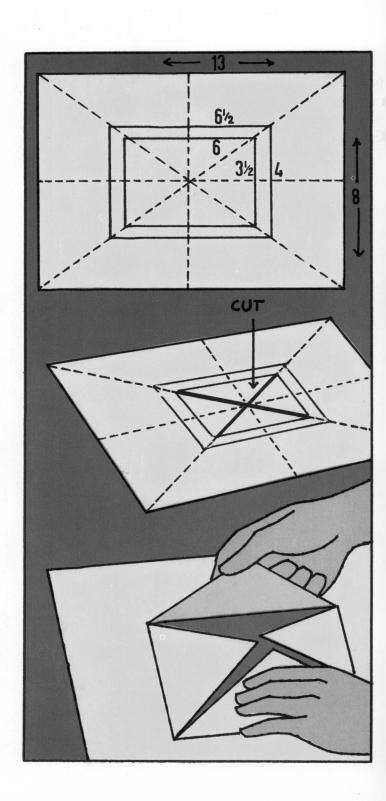

Cut a rectangle 13in. by 8in. out of cream card. Draw the lines shown in the picture by dotted lines on the back of the card.

Using the diagonal lines as a guide, draw two rectangles in the middle, one 6½in. by 4in., the other 6in. by 3½in. Score round the rectangles with the point of a pair of scissors.

Cut along the diagonals of the middle rectangle.

Fold out the four triangular flaps and glue them to the back of the card.

158

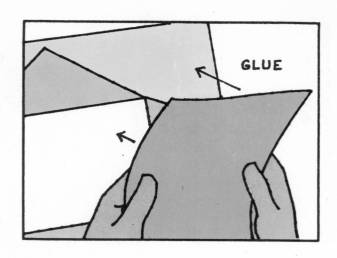

Now add a border to the frame, using a strip ¼in. wide cut out of a brightly coloured card.

Glue the picture in place on the back of the card.

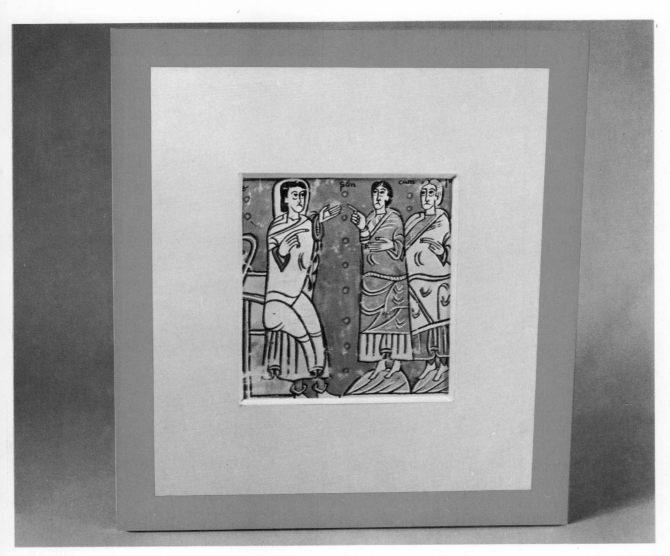

RELIEF WITH CIRCLE

Cut a 15in. square out of cardboard. Draw the diagonals to find the middle.

Cut a circle with a radius of 2in. out of metallic card, and another with a radius of 1in. out of black card. Stick them one on top of the other in the middle of the square.

Glue a strip of cardboard 12in. by 1½in. round the big circle as shown. Glue another four strips folded at right angles, 2in. away from the circle.

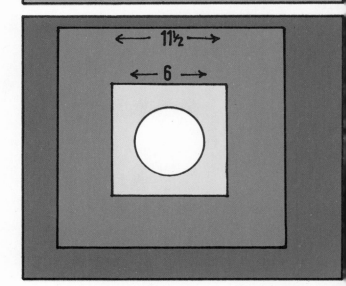

Cut an 11½in. square out of green card.
Glue a 6in. silver square inside the green one, keeping it in the middle.
Cut a circle with a radius of 1½in. out of the silver square.

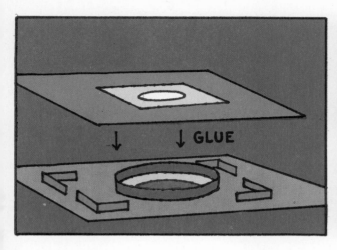 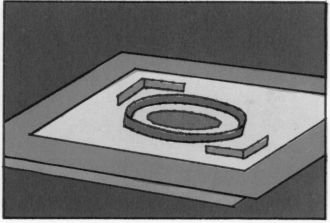

Glue the green and silver squares on to the top edges of the four strips.

Glue a strip of cardboard 15in. by $\frac{3}{4}$in. round the hole on the top square, 1in. away from the edge of the hole. Now glue two strips 9in. by $\frac{3}{4}$in. bent into right angles, about $1\frac{1}{2}$in. away from the circular strip.

Cut a $10\frac{1}{2}$in. square out of pink card and decorate as before, this time using a 7in. silver square and cutting out a circle with a radius of 2in.
Glue them on the upright strips. Stick another strip $22\frac{1}{2}$in. by $\frac{3}{4}$in. round the circle, $1\frac{1}{2}$in. away. Now cut a circle with a $2\frac{1}{2}$in. radius out of a $9\frac{1}{2}$in. square of white card, and stick the square on top of the others.

MATERIALS:

- Black and blue card and metallic card or paper
- Glue
- Scissors
- Pencil
- Ruler

RELIEF IN SILVER AND BLU

Cut a rectangle 13in. by 10½in. out of black card.

Cut twelve strips 10in. long out of blue card and twelve out of metallic card. Fold all the strips in half lengthwise.
Stick one blue strip to one silver one as shown in the drawing, until you have twelve pairs.

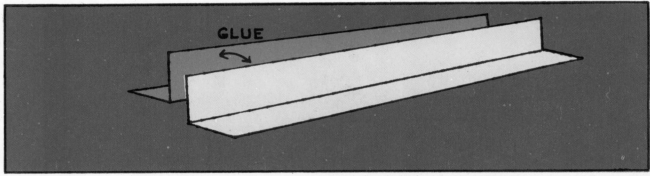

Glue these pairs on black card, alternating the colours and keeping the same margin all the way round.

Draw two circles one inside the other on black card. One has a radius of 6¼in., the other 6¾in. Cut out the ring they form.

Place the ring centrally over the strips and make a mark where the inside and outside edges of the ring touch the strips.

Cut out the spaces between the marks so the ring lies flat on the bottom of the strips. Glue it down.

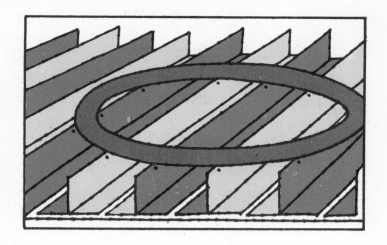

When the glue is quite dry, press the strips that are outside the black ring in one direction, and the strips inside the ring in the opposite direction.

BOAT

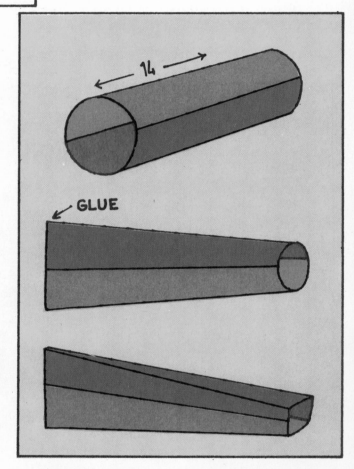

Cut two rectangles 14in. by 5in. out of red and black card. Glue the long edges together to make a cylinder.

Flatten one end of the cylinder so that the two colours show on either side. Glue the flattened ends to make the bow of the boat.

Press the other end of the cylinder into a rectangle 3½in. by 1in. as shown.

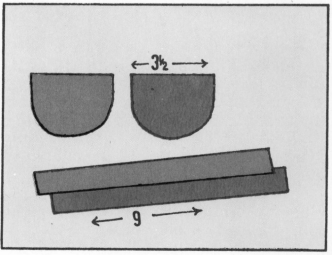

Cut a red and black piece 3½in. across in the shape of a heel of a shoe, of the same width as the base of the previous rectangle.

Glue the top edges of the pieces to the top and bottom of the rectangles, matching the colours.

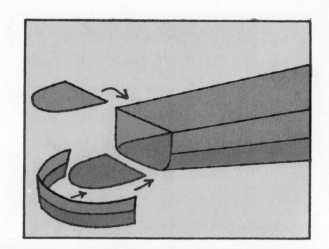

Cut a red and a black strip 9in. by ½in. Stick them together lengthwise. Glue them round the edge of the heel-shaped pieces to make the stern.

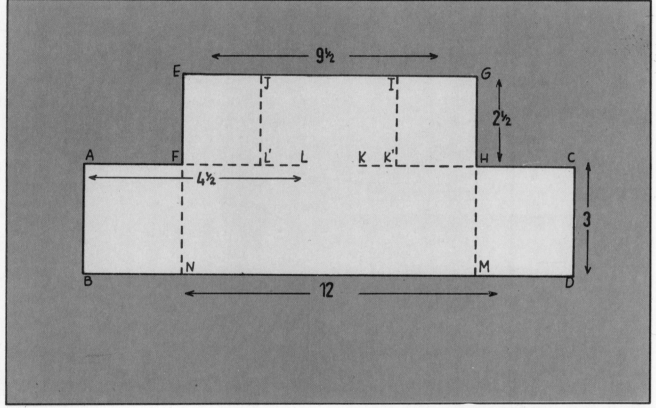

To make the captain's bridge, cut out a piece of white card following the instructions in the picture. Cut HK and FL, then make folds at HM, IK' JL' and FN.
Overlap flaps AB and CD and glue. Glue EF on GH.

Glue the bridge in the centre of the boat with a few strips placed on the inside of the bridge.

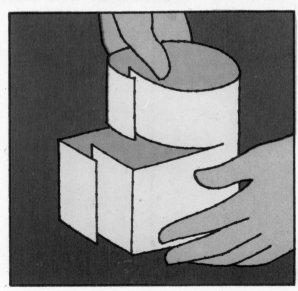

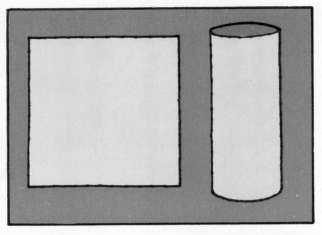

Cut a 5in. square out of blue card. Glue two sides together to form a cylinder for the funnel. Glue a $\frac{1}{2}$in. green strip round the funnel, $\frac{1}{2}$in. from the top.

Cut a rectangle 2$\frac{1}{2}$in. by 1$\frac{1}{2}$in. and glue one of the short sides down a strip of card 3in. by $\frac{1}{2}$in.
Glue the mast at the end of the stern. Finish the flag by gluing on an emblem in a different coloured card.

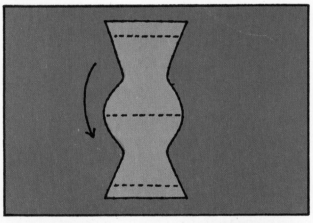

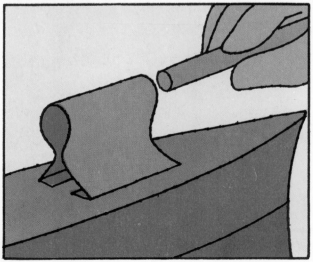

Cut a piece of grey card in the shape shown left. Fold along the dotted lines and bend the top part into a cylinder. Roll up a piece of grey card and glue one end inside the cylinder to make the cannon.
Glue the cannon on the bow of the boat.

Draw windows and a door on the bridge to finish the boat.

MATERIALS:

- Different coloured card
- Silver paper
- Scissors
- Ruler
- Pencil
- Glue
- Wire

BUGATTI

Cut a rectangle 12½in. by 10in. out of green card.

Glue the long ends together. Fold along the dotted lines and flatten out the base.

Make a cut at the top and bottom on both sides of the back.

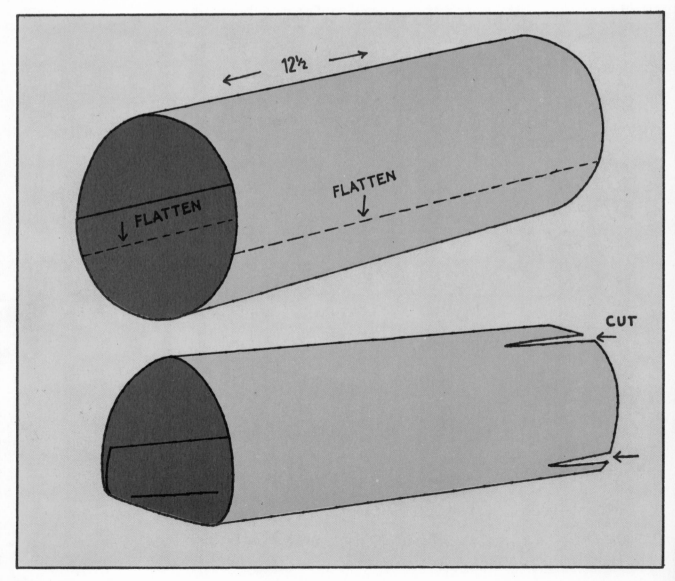

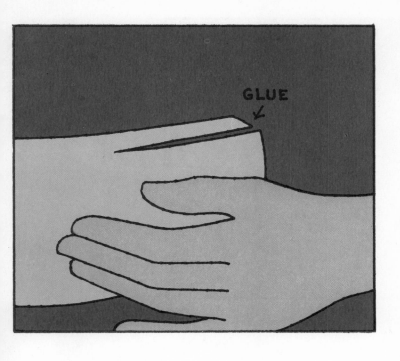

GLUE

Overlap the cut edges to taper the end of the cylinder, and glue.

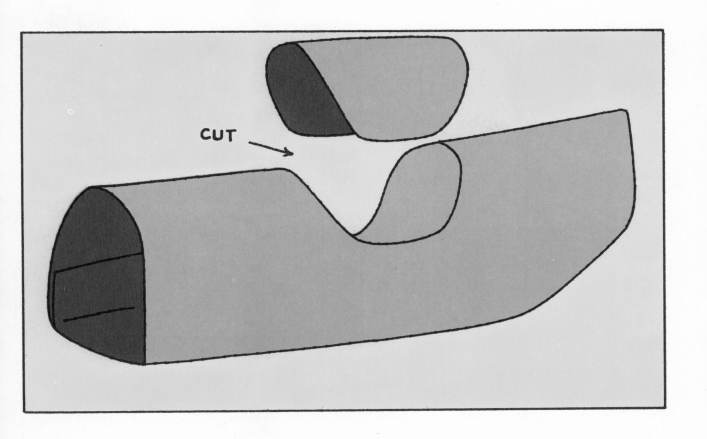

CUT

Cut this shape out of the top of the body to make a space for the driver's seat.

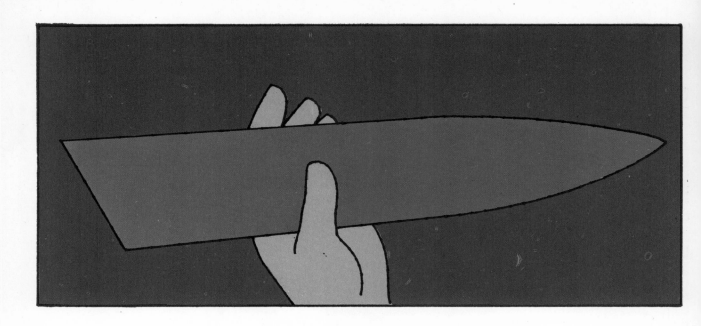

Cut out a piece of grey card like this and glue underneath the car.

To make the wheels, cut four circles with a radius of 1½in. out of black card.
Cut another four circles with a radius of 1in. out of metallic card.
Glue each metallic circle on a black one.

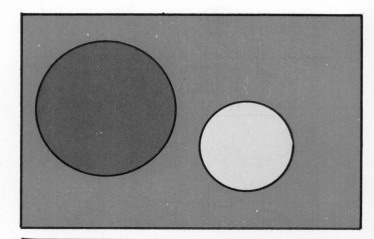

Cut two rectangles out of grey card for the axles. Fold along the dotted lines.

Glue the ends to make two hollow triangular shapes.

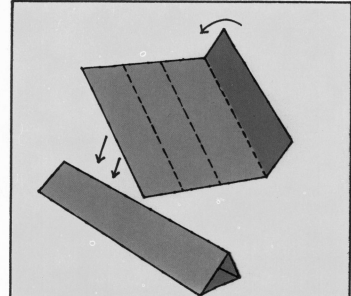

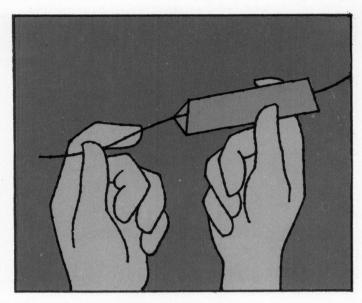

Thread a wire through each of the triangles.

Glue them underneath the car at the front and back.

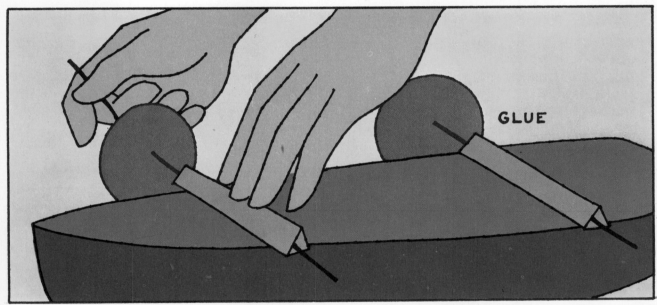

GLUE

Push the ends of the wires through the middle of the wheels.

Bend the ends into a spiral to hold the wheels in place.

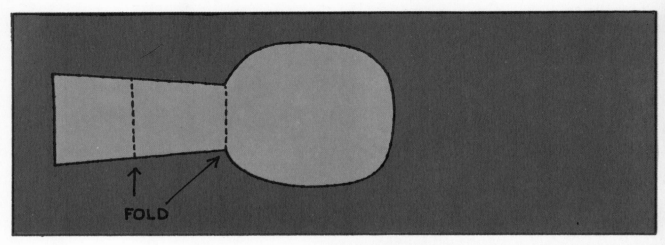

The seat is made out of grey card. Cut out a piece like this, making it as wide as the driving compartment. Fold along the dotted lines and glue it inside the car.
Cut a semicircle with a few flaps out of red card.
Fold down the flaps and glue in position.
Make a steering wheel out of a piece of wire and push it into the dashboard.

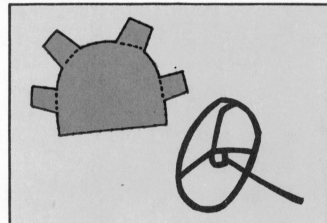

The radiator is made up of three sections:

No. 1 is in yellow card.

No. 2 is in silver paper.

No. 3, in silver paper, fits over the flaps on the first piece.

Glue them in this order on the front of the car.

INDEX